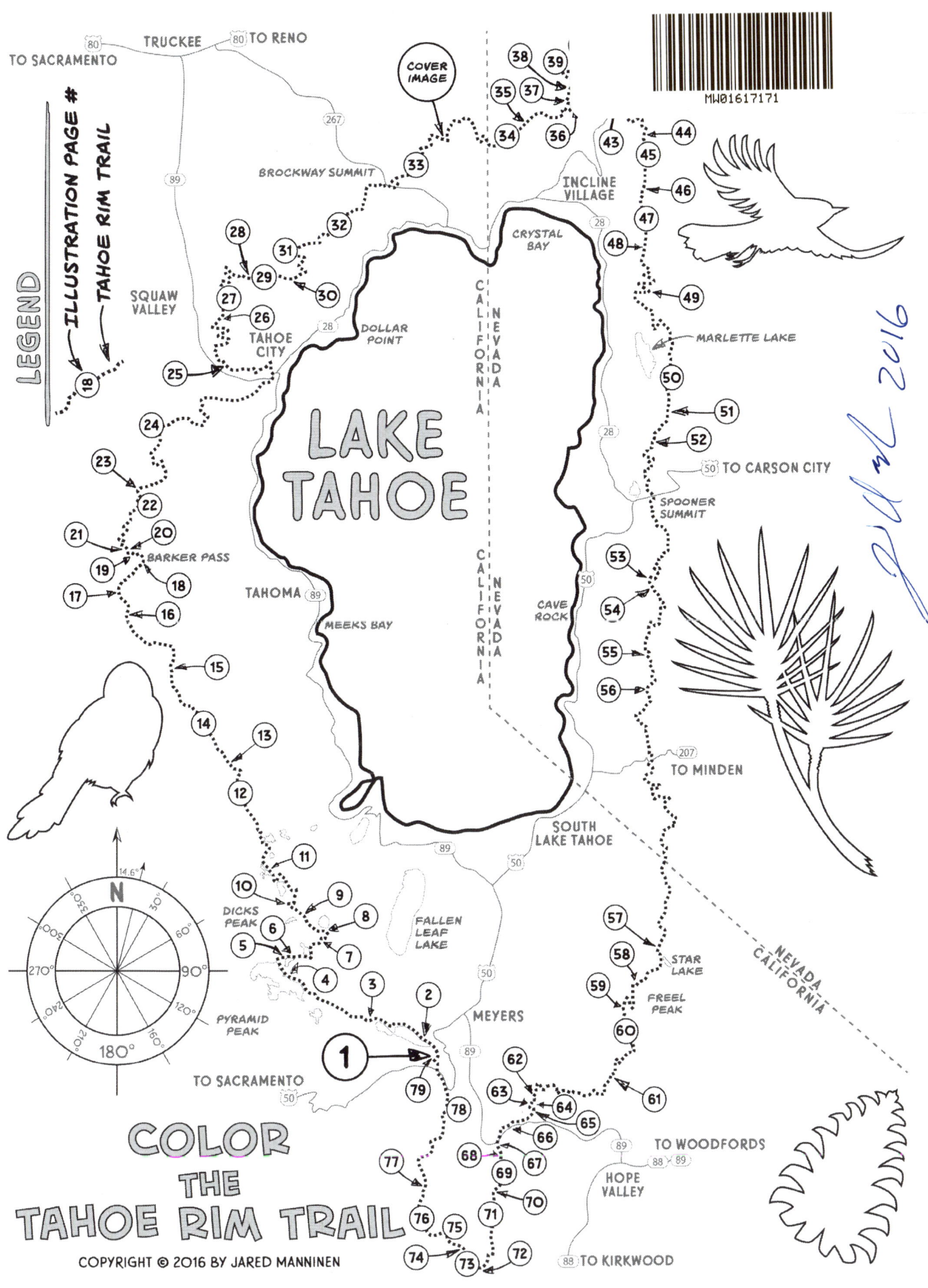

COLOR
THE
TAHOE RIM TRAIL

COPYRIGHT © 2016 BY JARED MANNINEN

What adventures have you been on lately? That is one of the first questions I would ask customers while working at a gear shop in South Lake Tahoe. People came from all over the world, so I'd hear some exciting answers. Many of the customers just chuckled and said something about their daily grind. When I dug a little deeper, however, most of those people did have an interesting story to tell. They just didn't view their experiences as "adventures" until I helped them re-frame their stories so they could see them through my eyes.

Conflict is at the heart of any adventure but it's not strictly limited to physical conflict, like you would find on an Everest expedition. Oftentimes the conflict is internal and the adventure revolves around overcoming a belief about yourself or a situation. **Adventure is a state of mind.** It's about learning new things and gaining a different perspective. To welcome adventure into your life is to embrace new challenges, adopt a "beginner's mind," and to let go of old beliefs that prevent you from seeing your life with a fresh set of eyes. So, what adventures have **you** been on lately?

Ways in which I incorporate adventure into my life:

- Acquire new skills by attending classes, seminars, and other educational courses.
- Learn about the history of where I live by visiting historical societies, museums, and libraries.
- Implement a framework or a set of rules for performing an activity or task to see where it takes me, such as cooking a meal with all the same colored ingredients or shapes.
- Ask waiters at restaurants to choose my meals lest I order the same thing over and over.
- Take different routes or modes of transportation to and from work, school, or the gym.
- Treat exploring as a lifestyle by taking multiple short trips instead of one big vacation each year. This approach isn't as immersive, but it's more affordable and easier to plan.
- Find on a map the most odd or uniquely named city, town, or location and travel to it.
- Get dropped off at trailheads and hike home. Sometimes the trip is a day-hike and other times it takes multiple days. I'm fortunate to live in a place where I have only short road walks to get to wilderness, but I do walk through neighborhoods if it's the most direct route.
- Document my experiences with photos, drawings, and journaling. These activities cause me to slow down and look more meaningfully at things.

Suggested approaches to coloring in this book:

- My drawing style is loose and scratchy and can be challenging to interpret, so study each illustration and plan out how you will color it. Treat the experience as a collaboration between the two of us and build upon the foundation I laid.
- Color and embellish the illustrations with various mediums, such as pencils, pens, markers, crayons, colored pencils, and watercolor pencils.
- Research each drawing's subject matter to determine accurate colors to use.
- Experiment with funky colors to create psychedelic and alien looking landscapes.

COLOR THE TAHOE RIM TRAIL

COLOR THE TAHOE RIM TRAIL WAS DESIGNED AND PUBLISHED IN SOUTH LAKE TAHOE, CALIFORNIA (NOVEMBER 2016)
COLOR THE TAHOE RIM TRAIL WAS PRINTED BY CREATESPACE, AN AMAZON.COM COMPANY
ALL FONTS USED IN *COLOR THE TAHOE RIM TRAIL* WERE CREATED BY NATE PIEKOS OF WWW.BLAMBOT.COM
ISBN: 978-0-9834036-5-4

FOR BONUS PAGES, TO POST PHOTOS OF YOUR COLORED PAGES, AND MORE INFO VISIT:
- WWW.WILDERNESSACTIVITYBOOKS.COM
- WWW.JAREDMANNINEN.COM

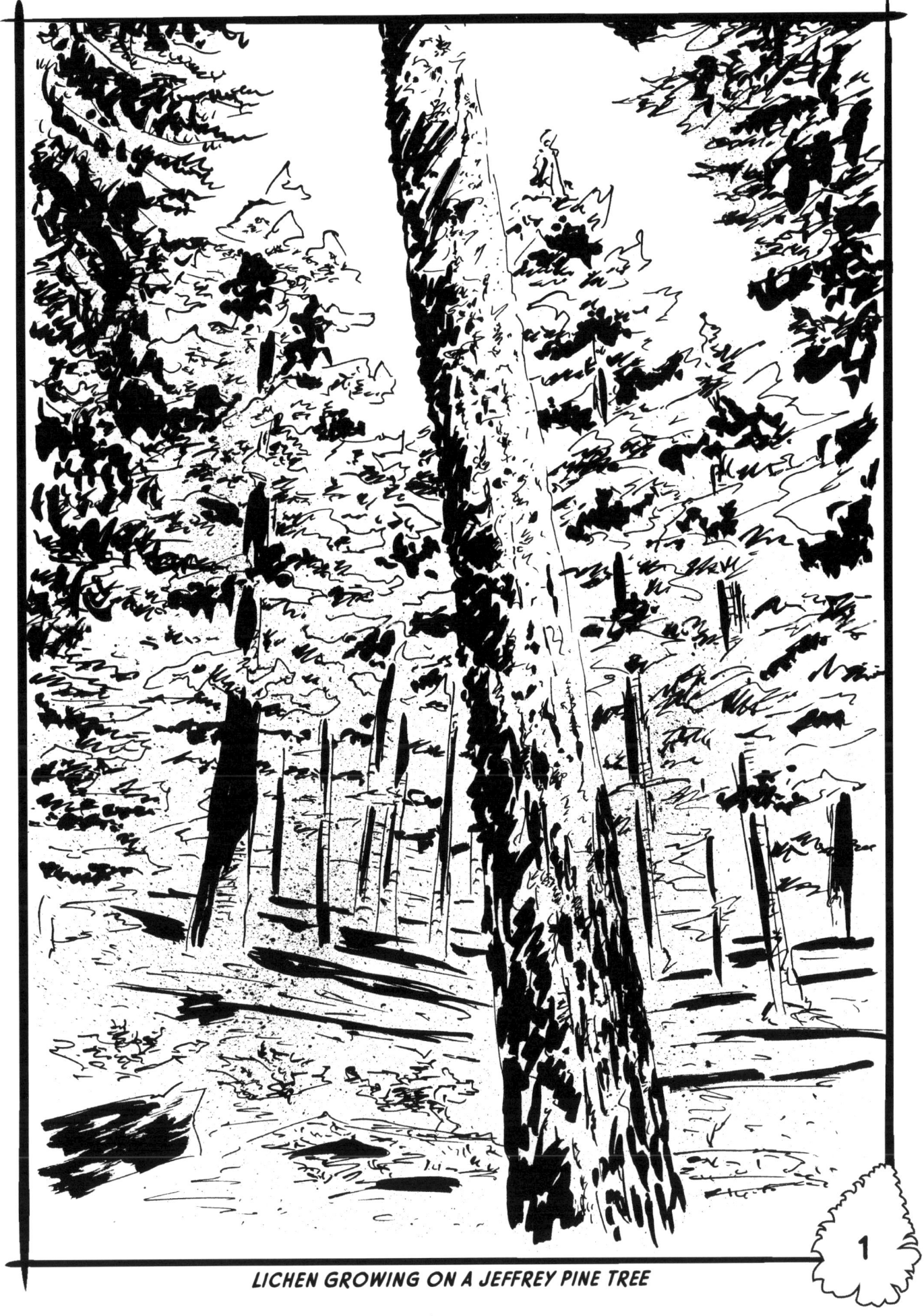

LICHEN GROWING ON A JEFFREY PINE TREE

1

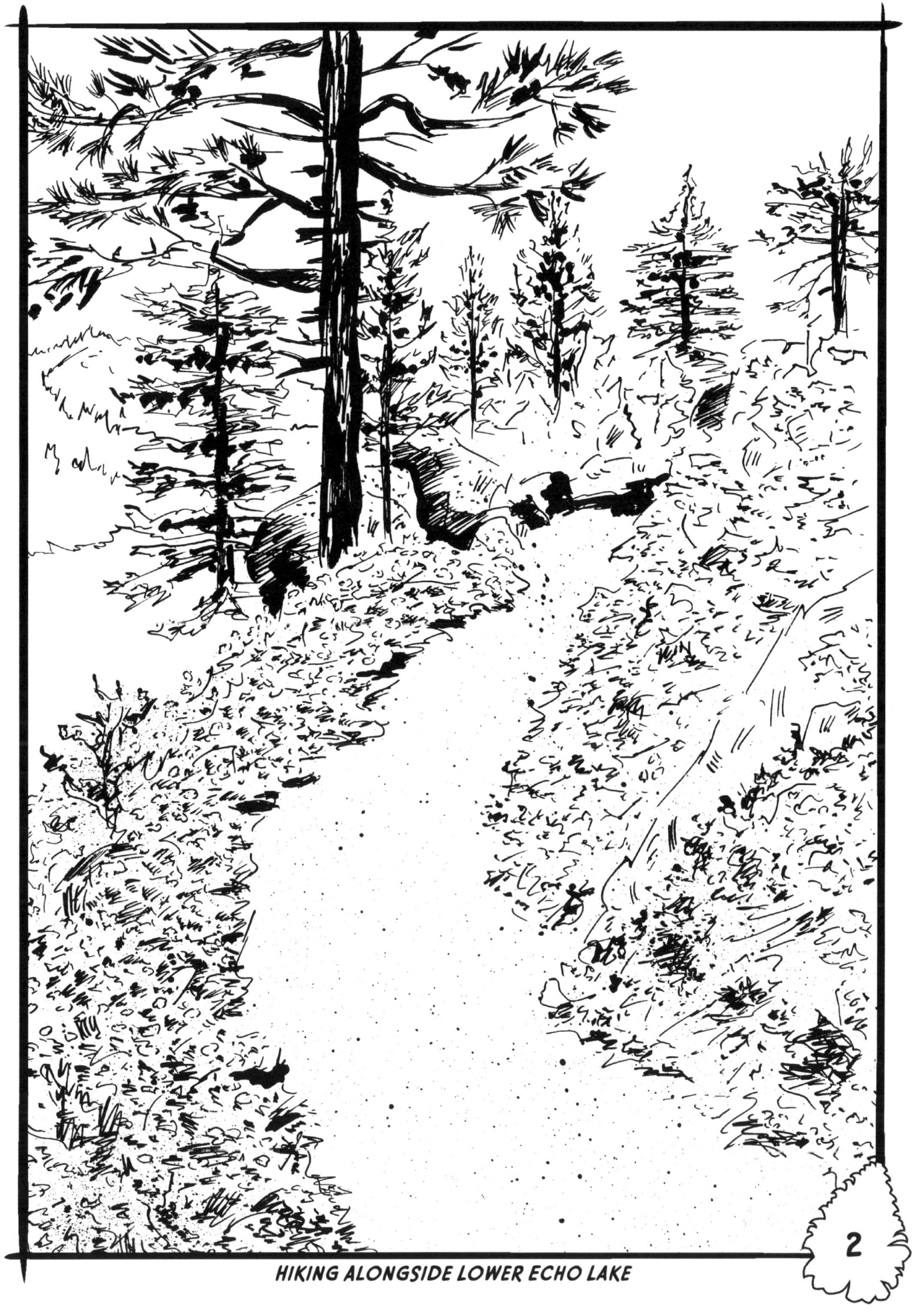

HIKING ALONGSIDE LOWER ECHO LAKE

2

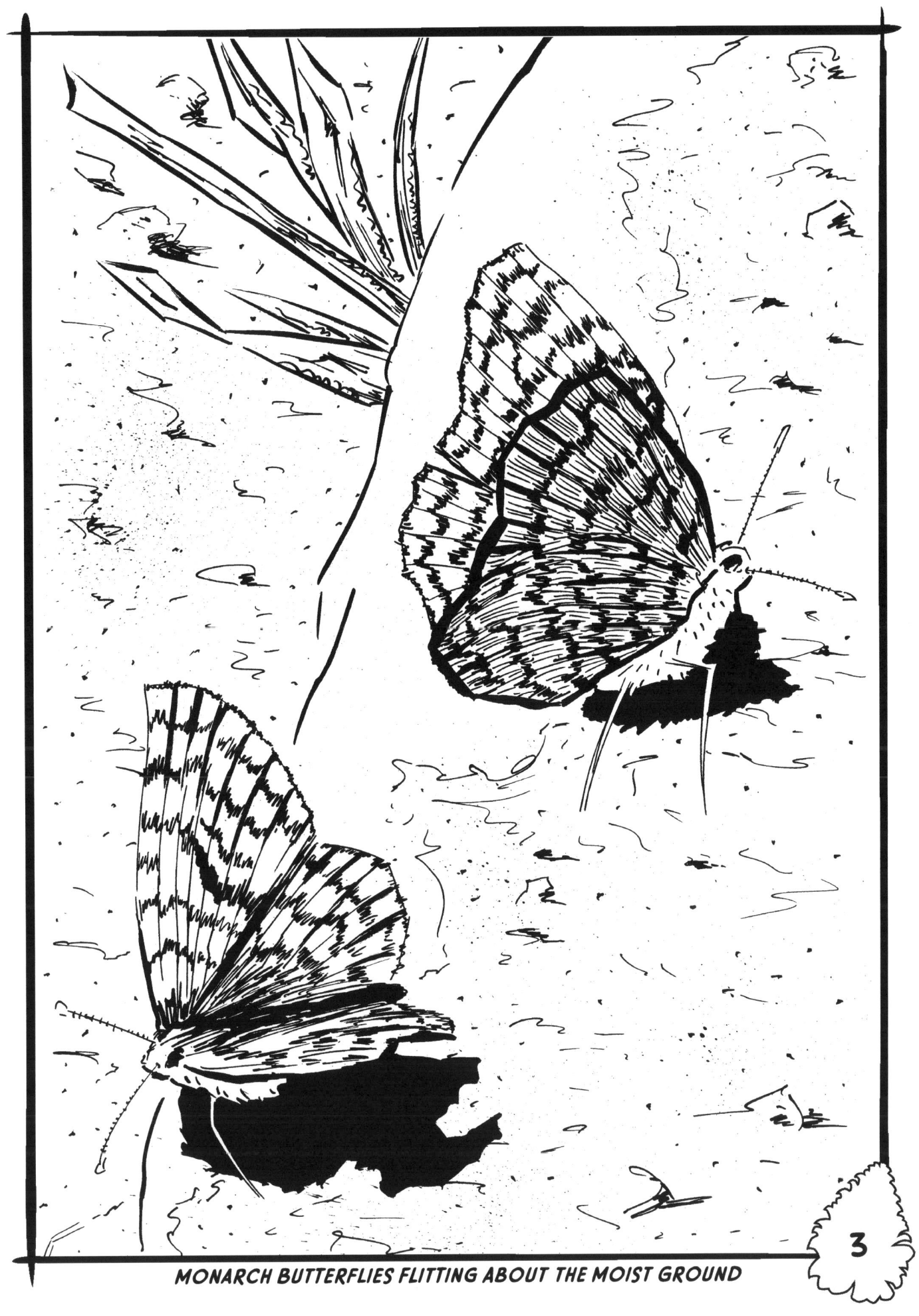

MONARCH BUTTERFLIES FLITTING ABOUT THE MOIST GROUND

3

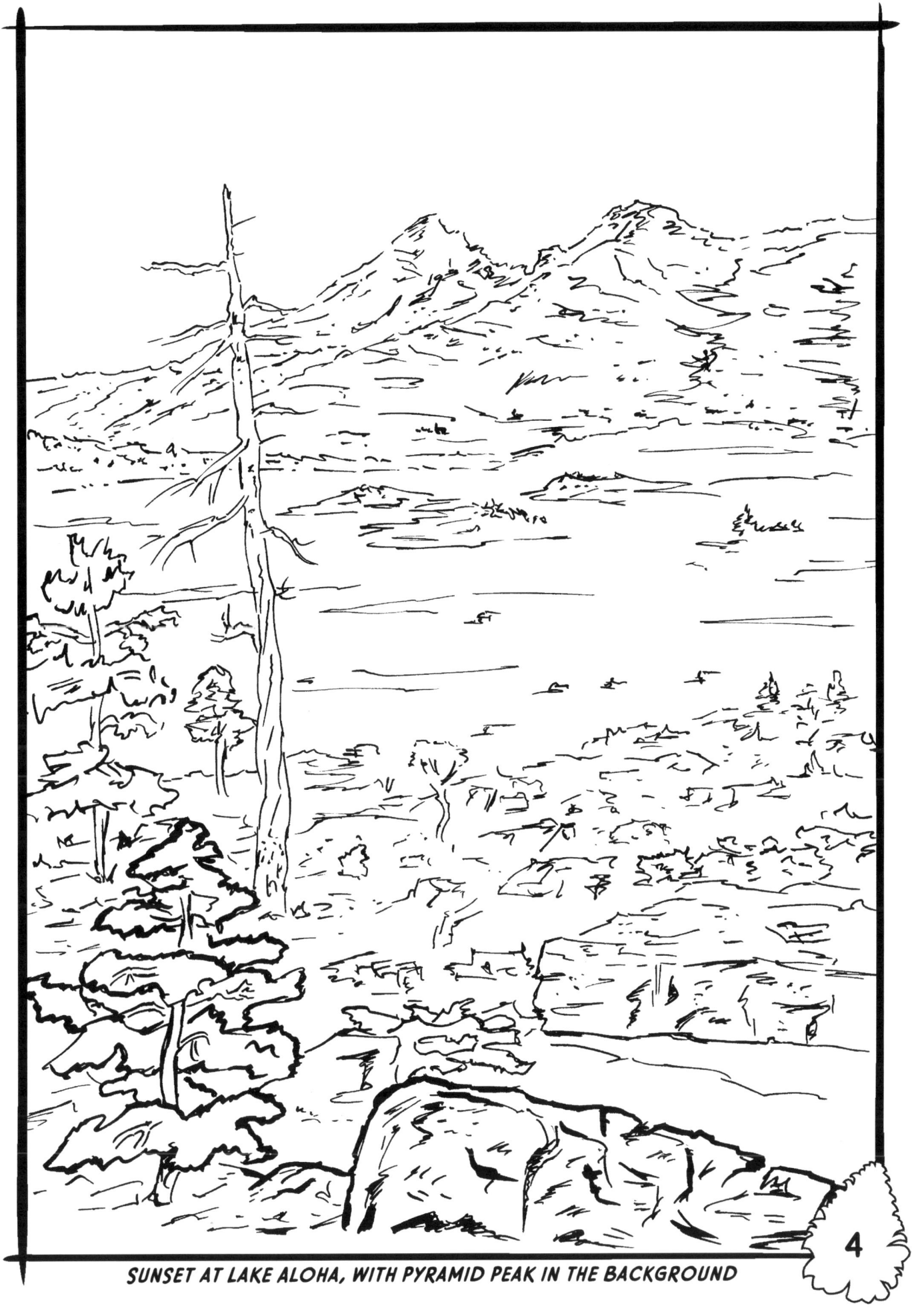

4

SUNSET AT LAKE ALOHA, WITH PYRAMID PEAK IN THE BACKGROUND

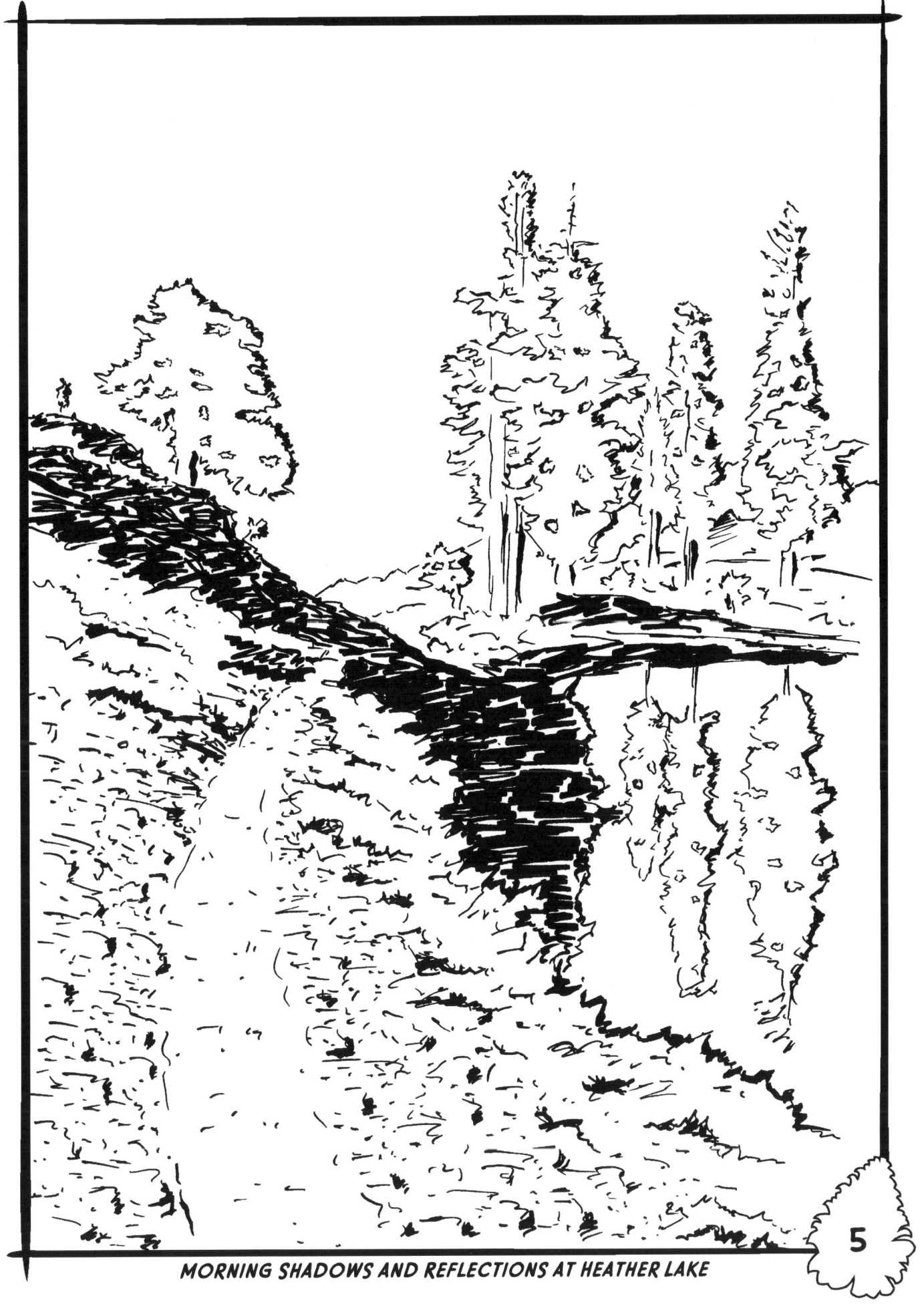

MORNING SHADOWS AND REFLECTIONS AT HEATHER LAKE

5

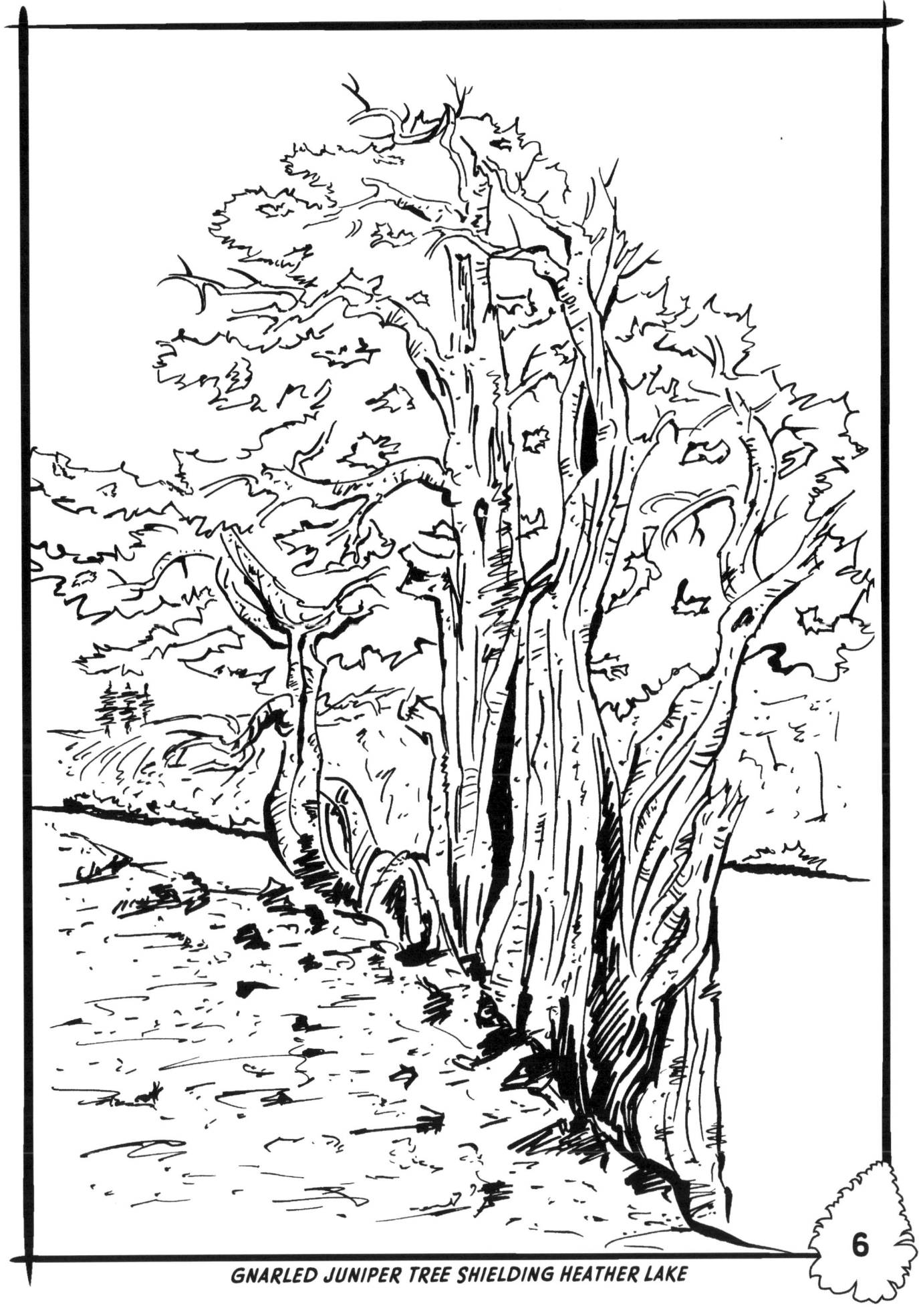

6

GNARLED JUNIPER TREE SHIELDING HEATHER LAKE

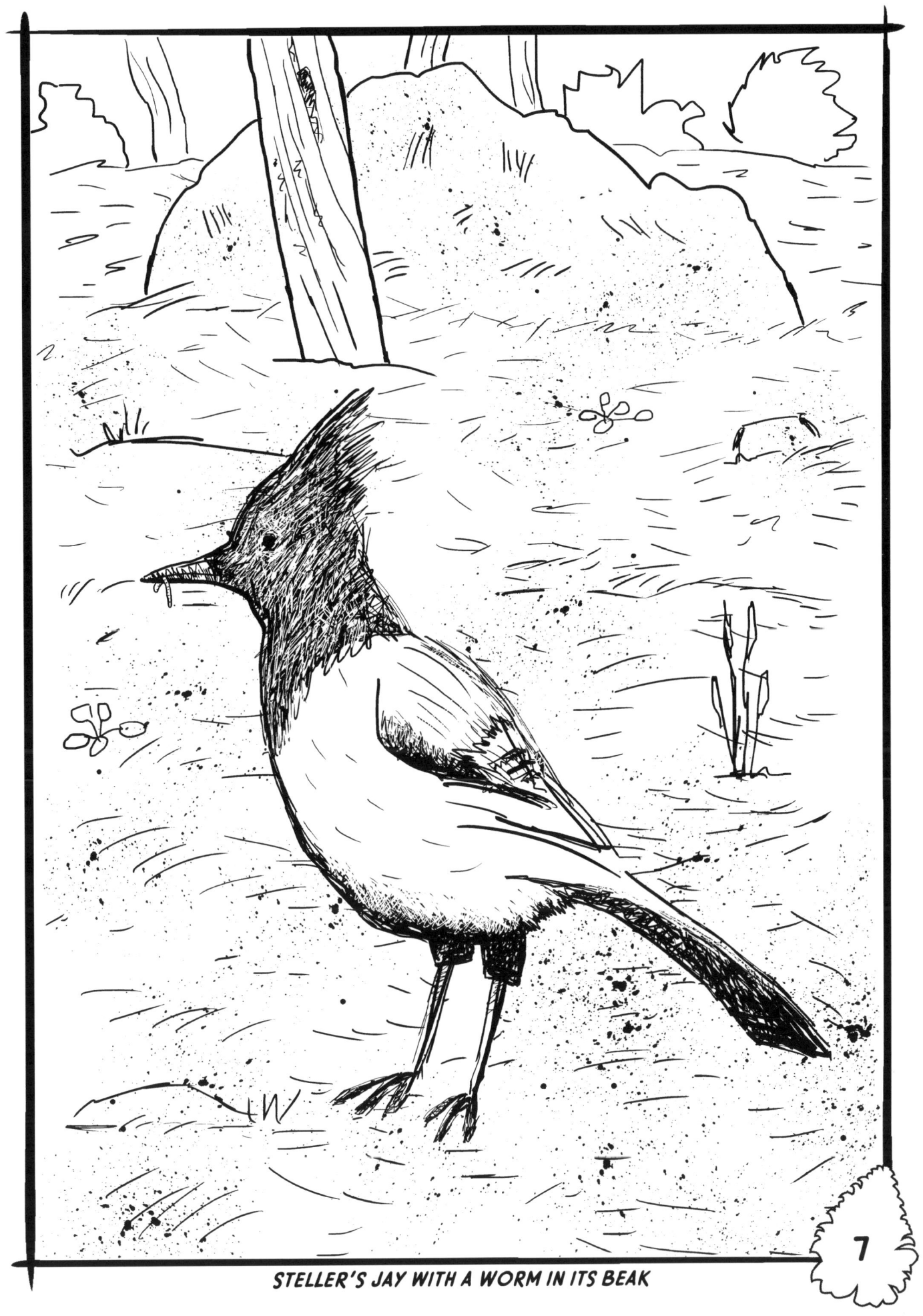

STELLER'S JAY WITH A WORM IN ITS BEAK

7

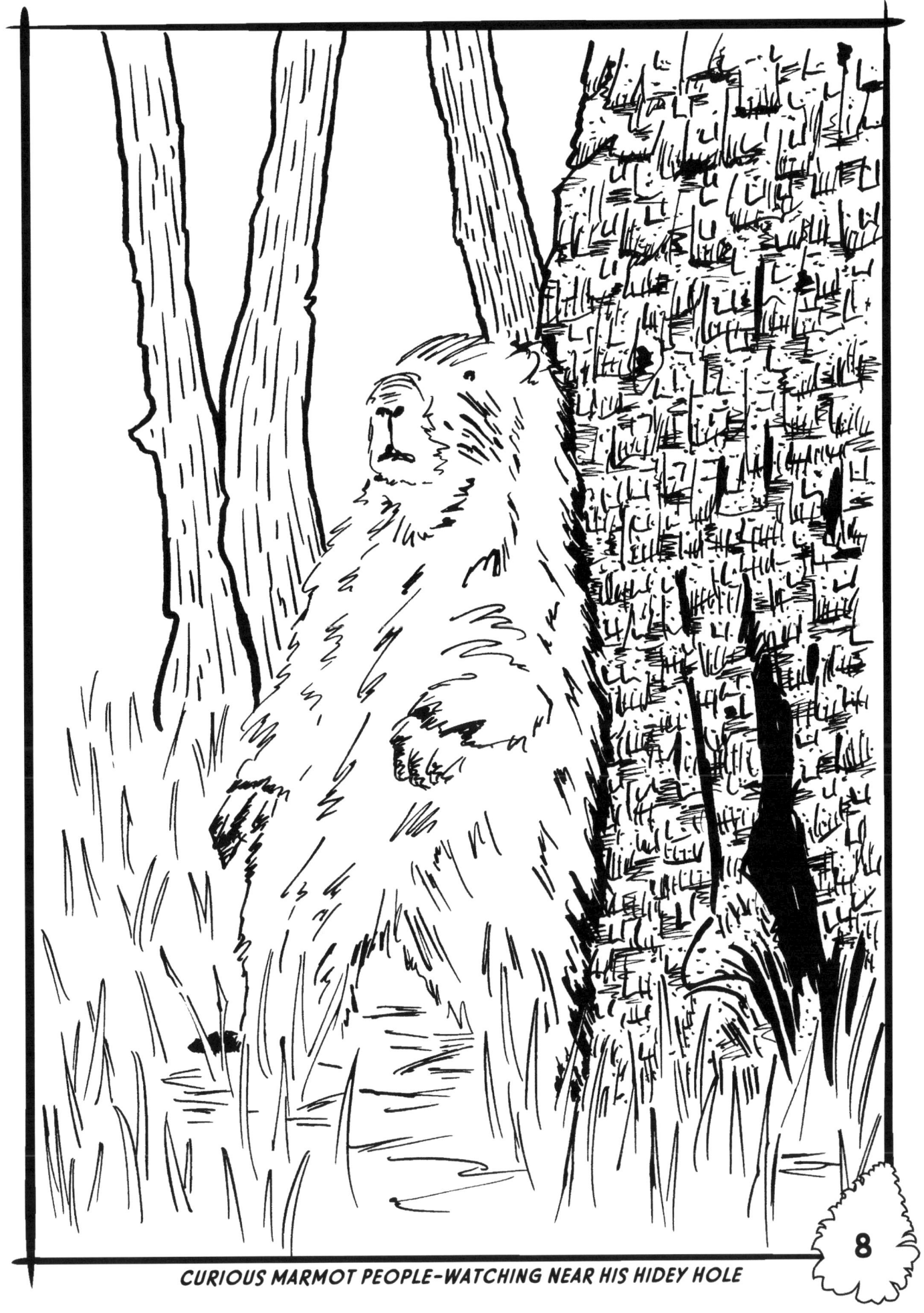

CURIOUS MARMOT PEOPLE-WATCHING NEAR HIS HIDEY HOLE

8

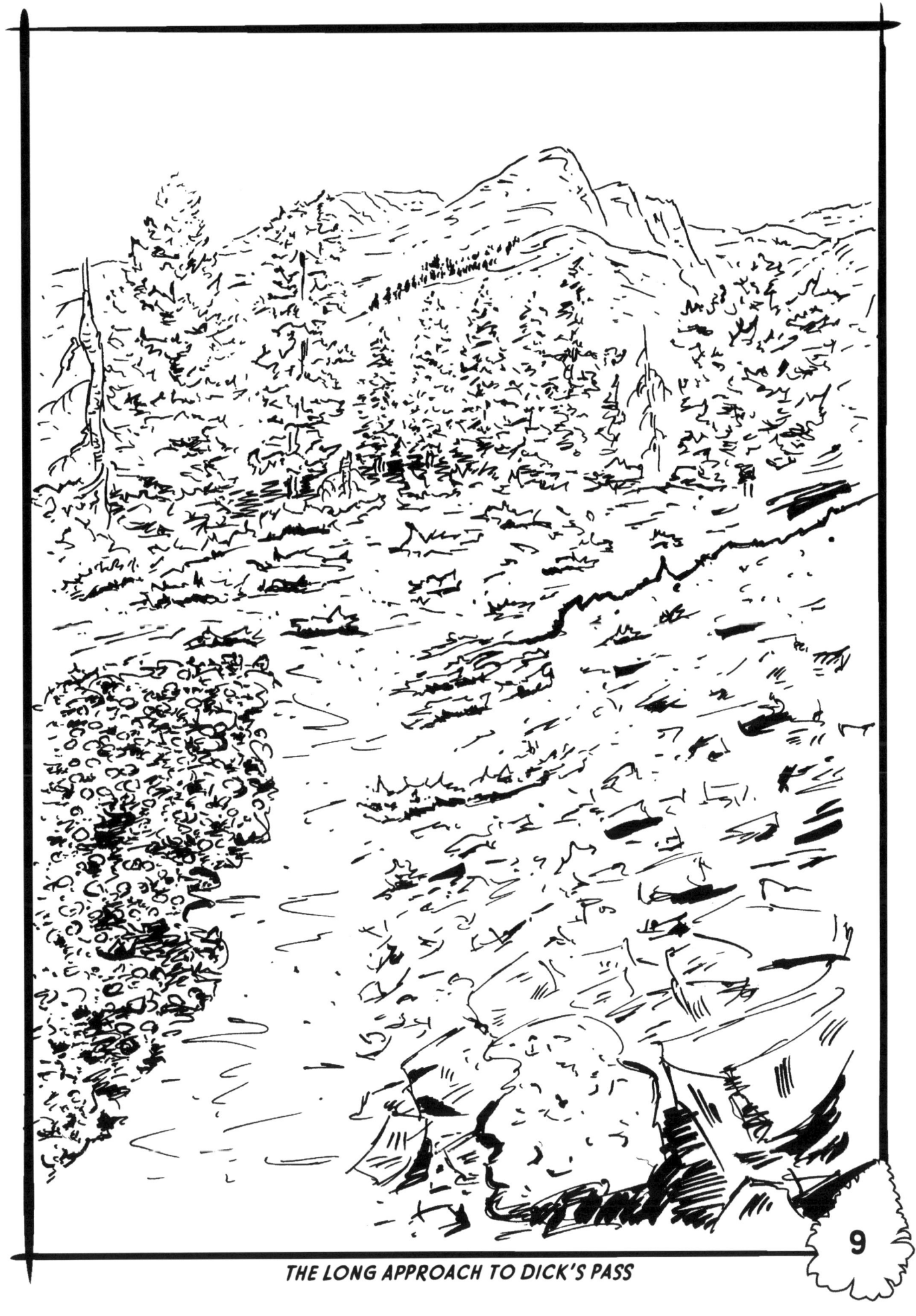

THE LONG APPROACH TO DICK'S PASS

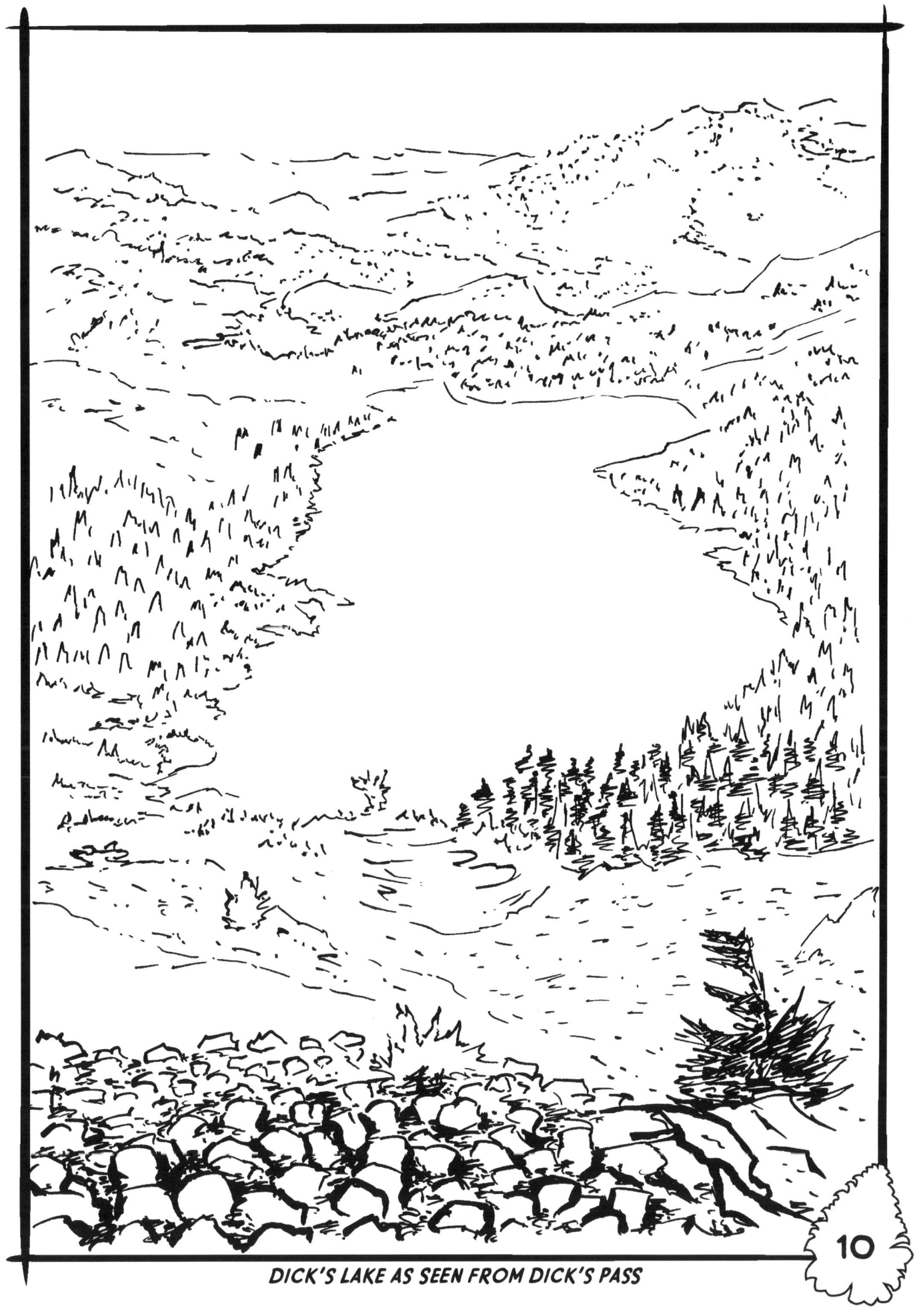

DICK'S LAKE AS SEEN FROM DICK'S PASS

10

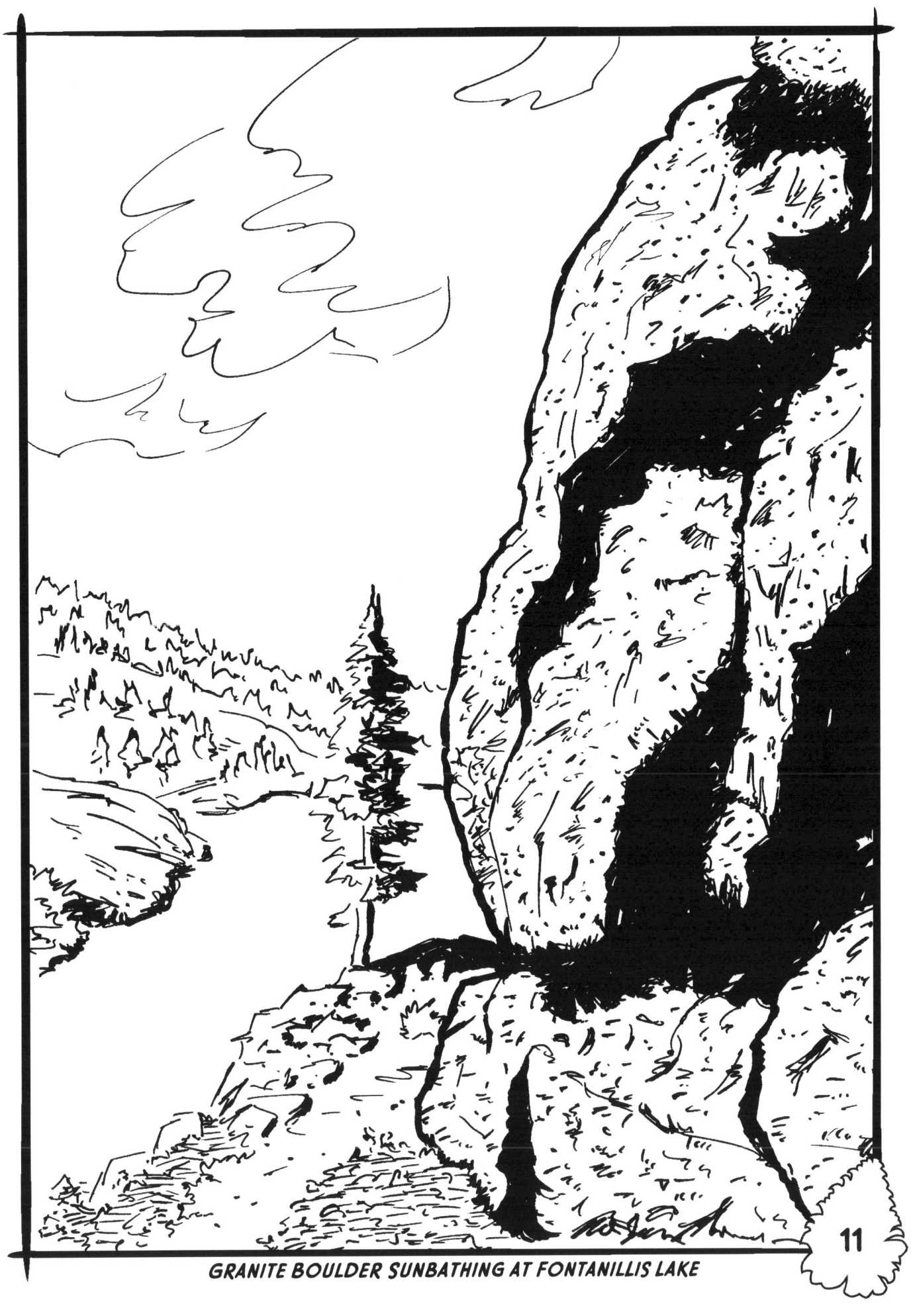

GRANITE BOULDER SUNBATHING AT FONTANILLIS LAKE

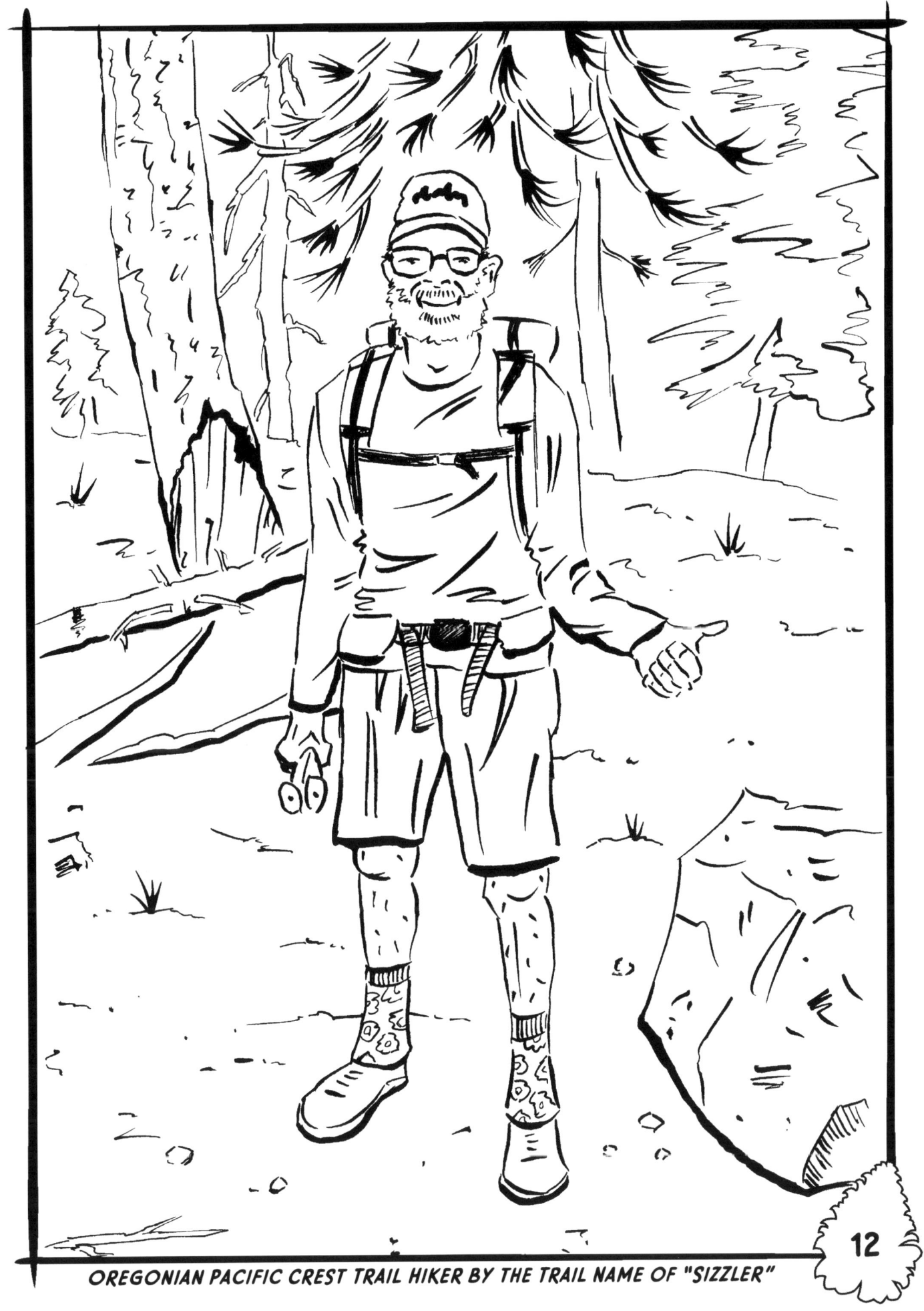

OREGONIAN PACIFIC CREST TRAIL HIKER BY THE TRAIL NAME OF "SIZZLER"

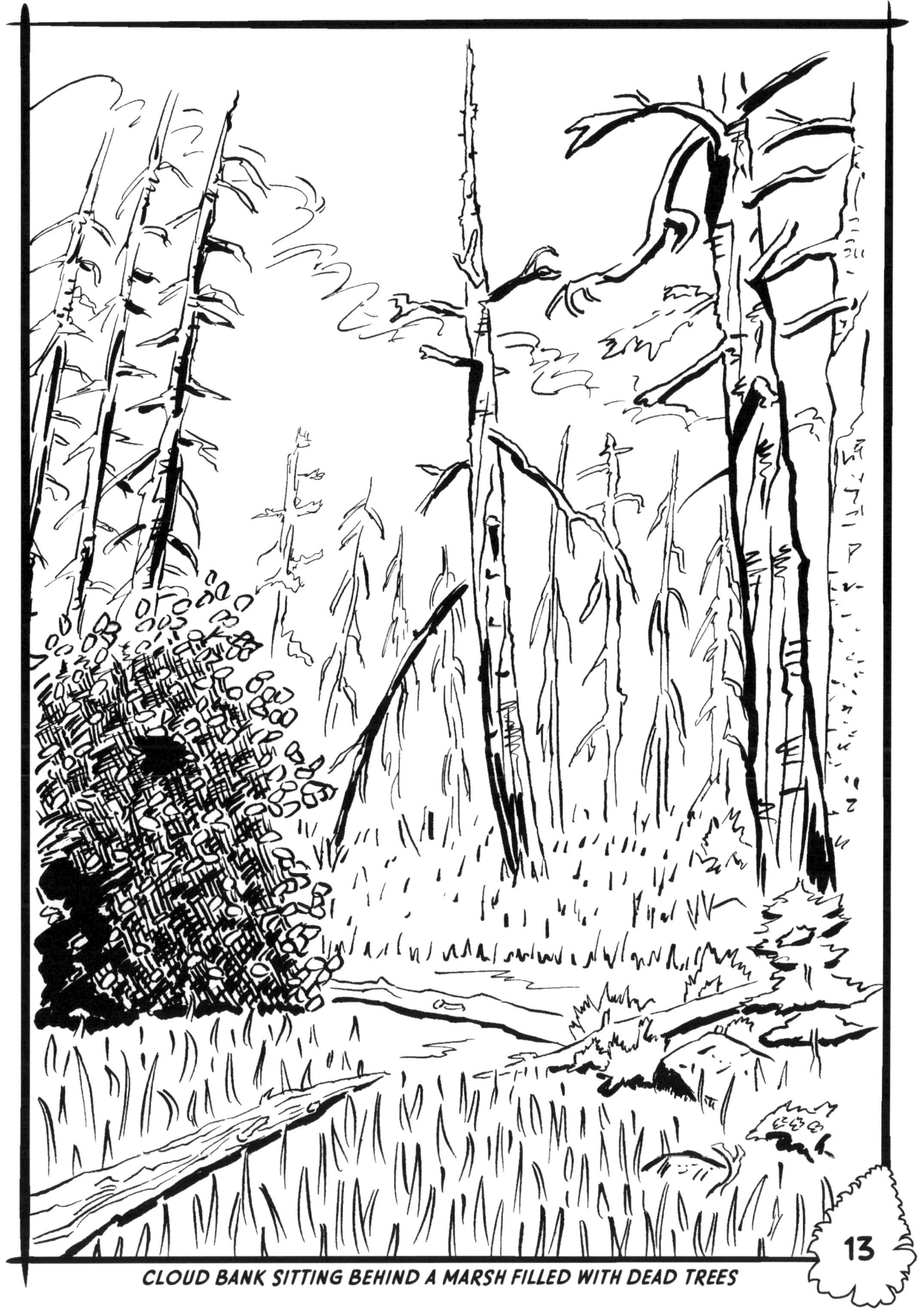

13

CLOUD BANK SITTING BEHIND A MARSH FILLED WITH DEAD TREES

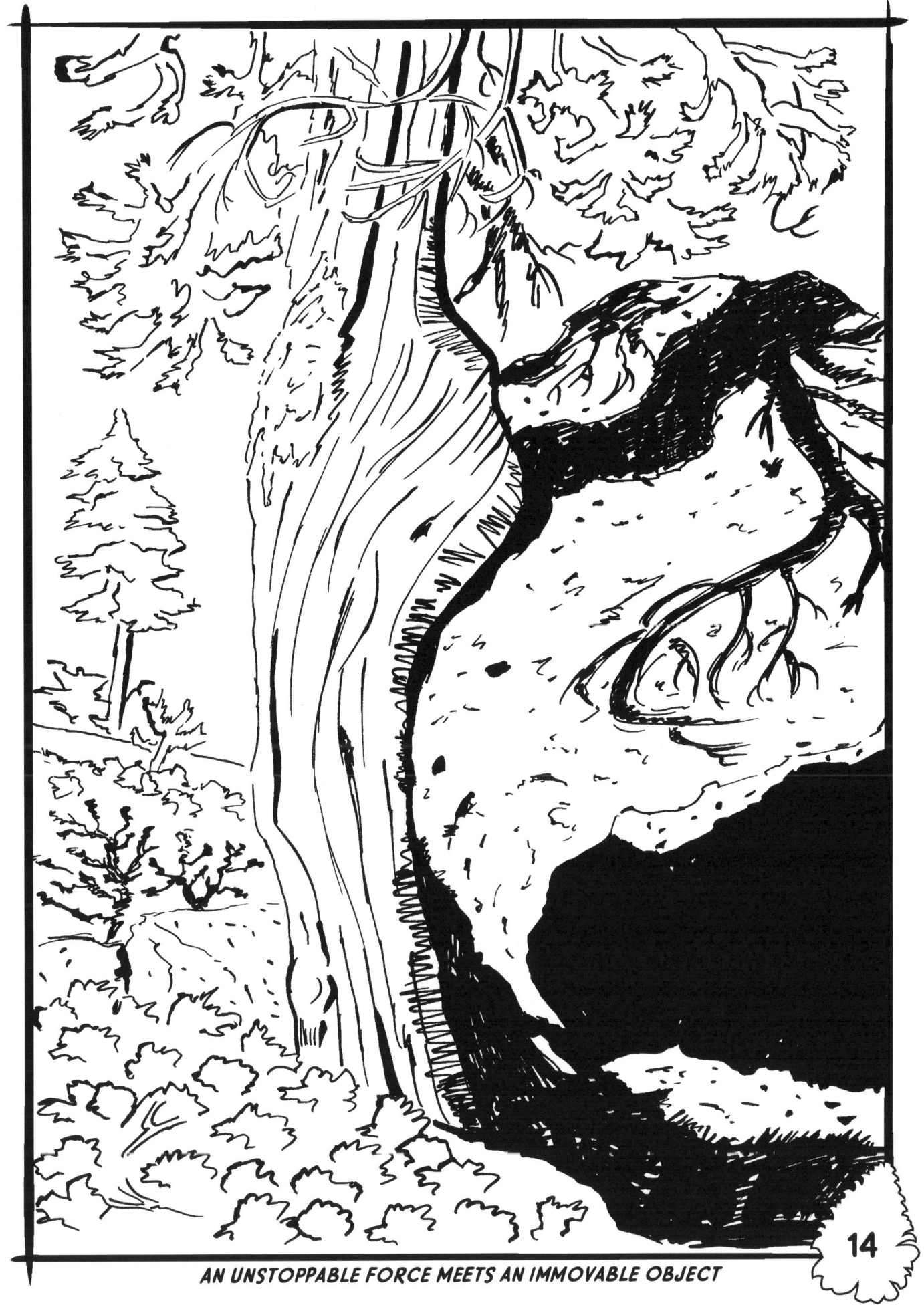

AN UNSTOPPABLE FORCE MEETS AN IMMOVABLE OBJECT

14

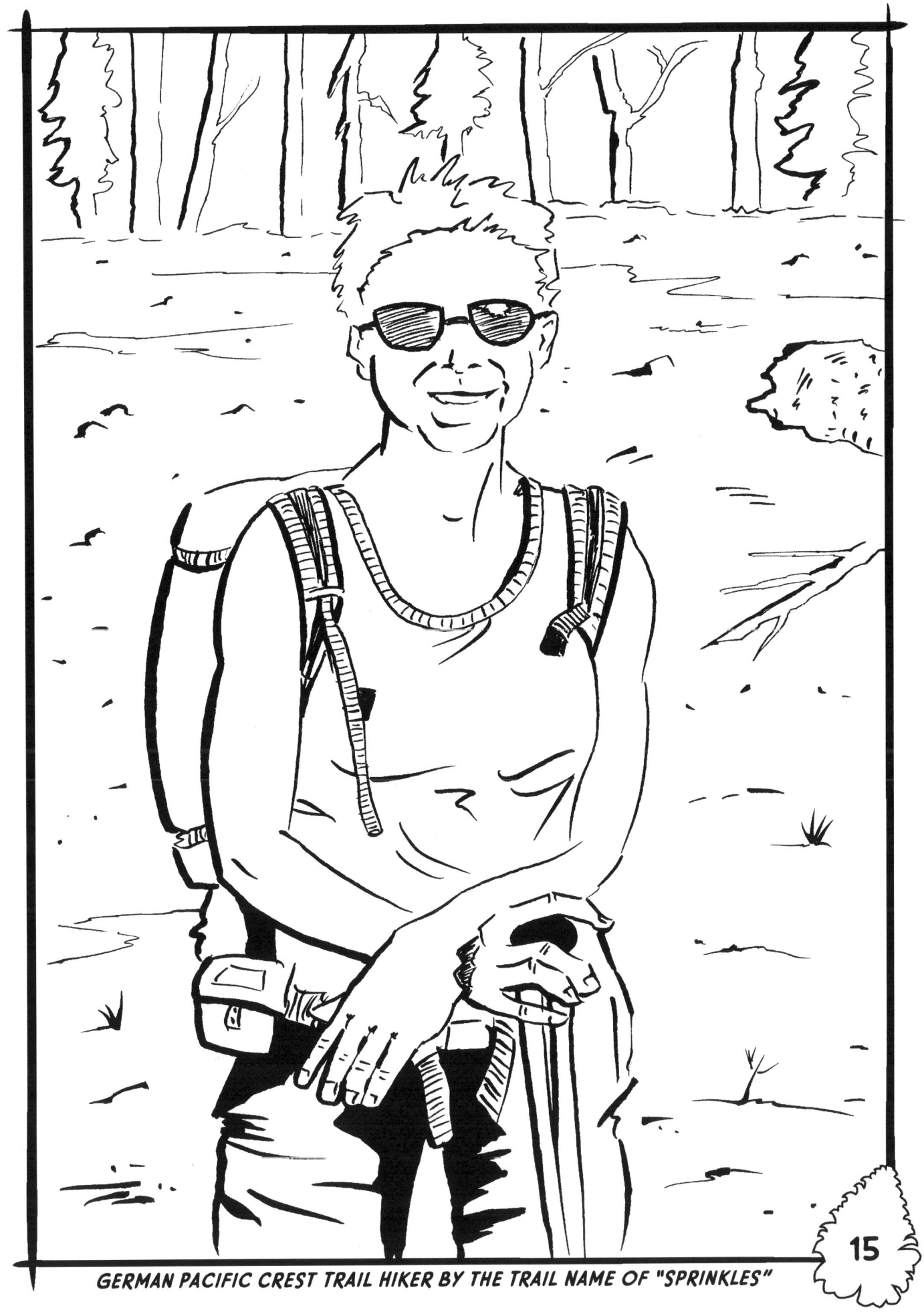

GERMAN PACIFIC CREST TRAIL HIKER BY THE TRAIL NAME OF "SPRINKLES"

15

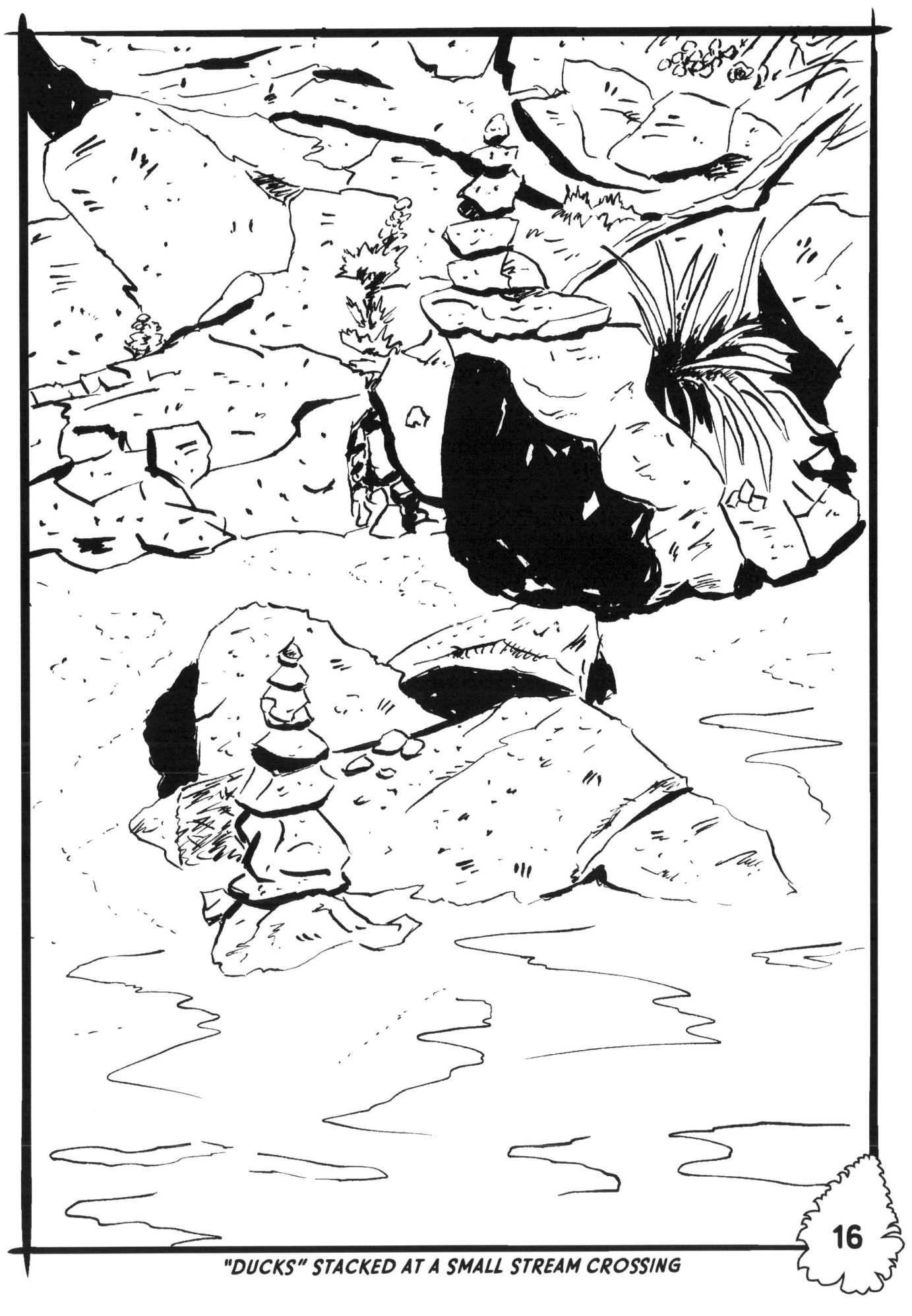

"DUCKS" STACKED AT A SMALL STREAM CROSSING

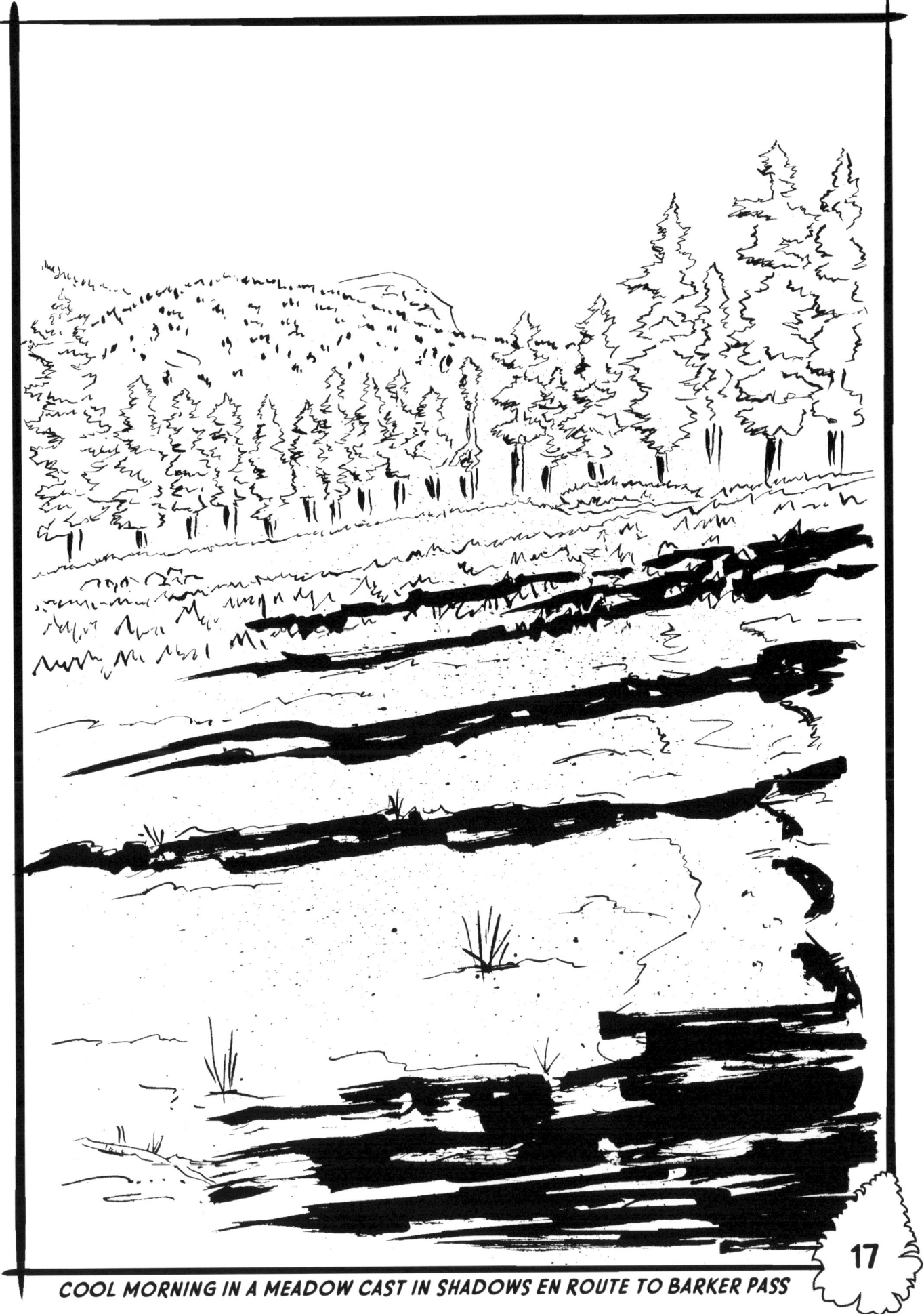

17

COOL MORNING IN A MEADOW CAST IN SHADOWS EN ROUTE TO BARKER PASS

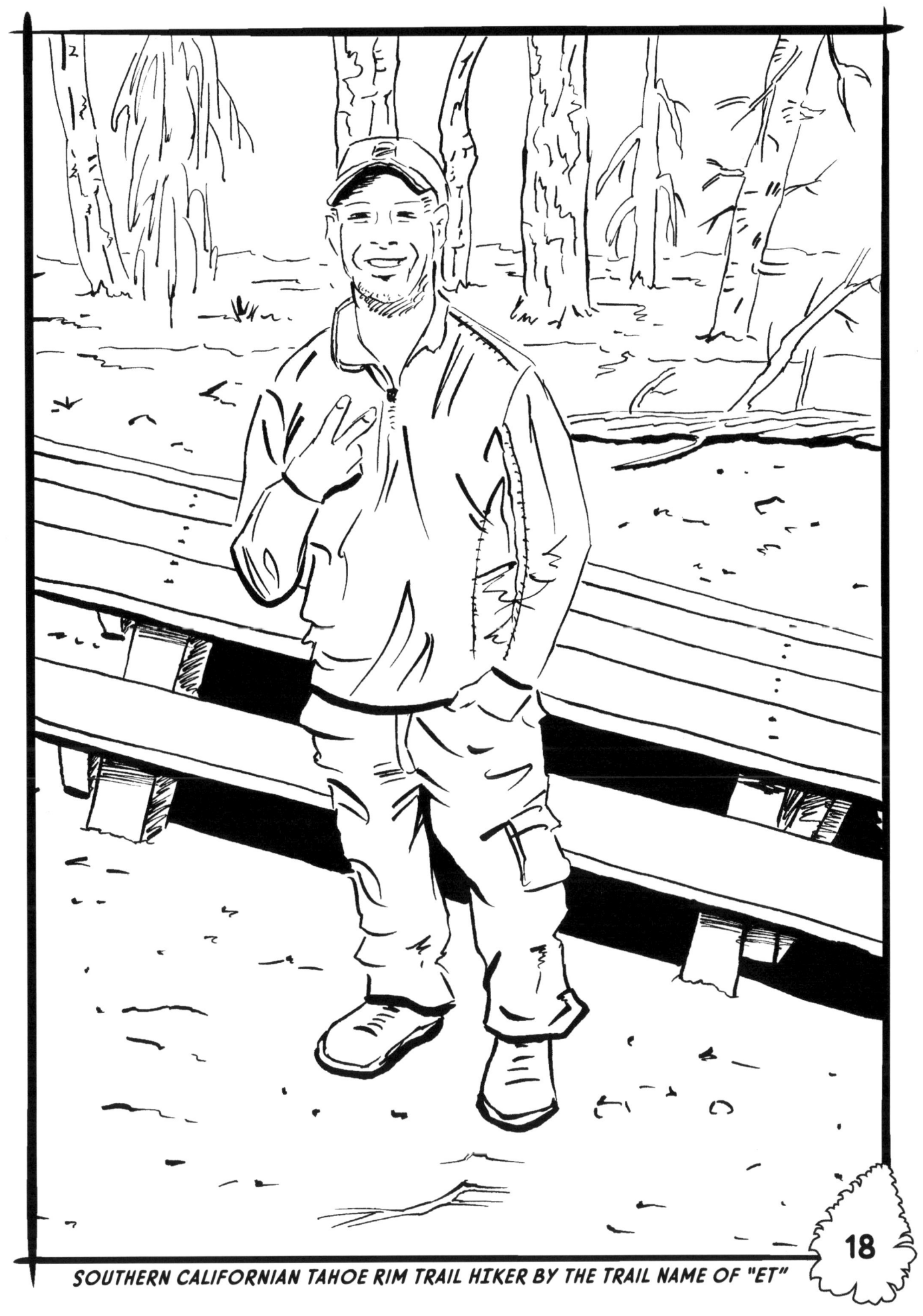

SOUTHERN CALIFORNIAN TAHOE RIM TRAIL HIKER BY THE TRAIL NAME OF "ET"

18

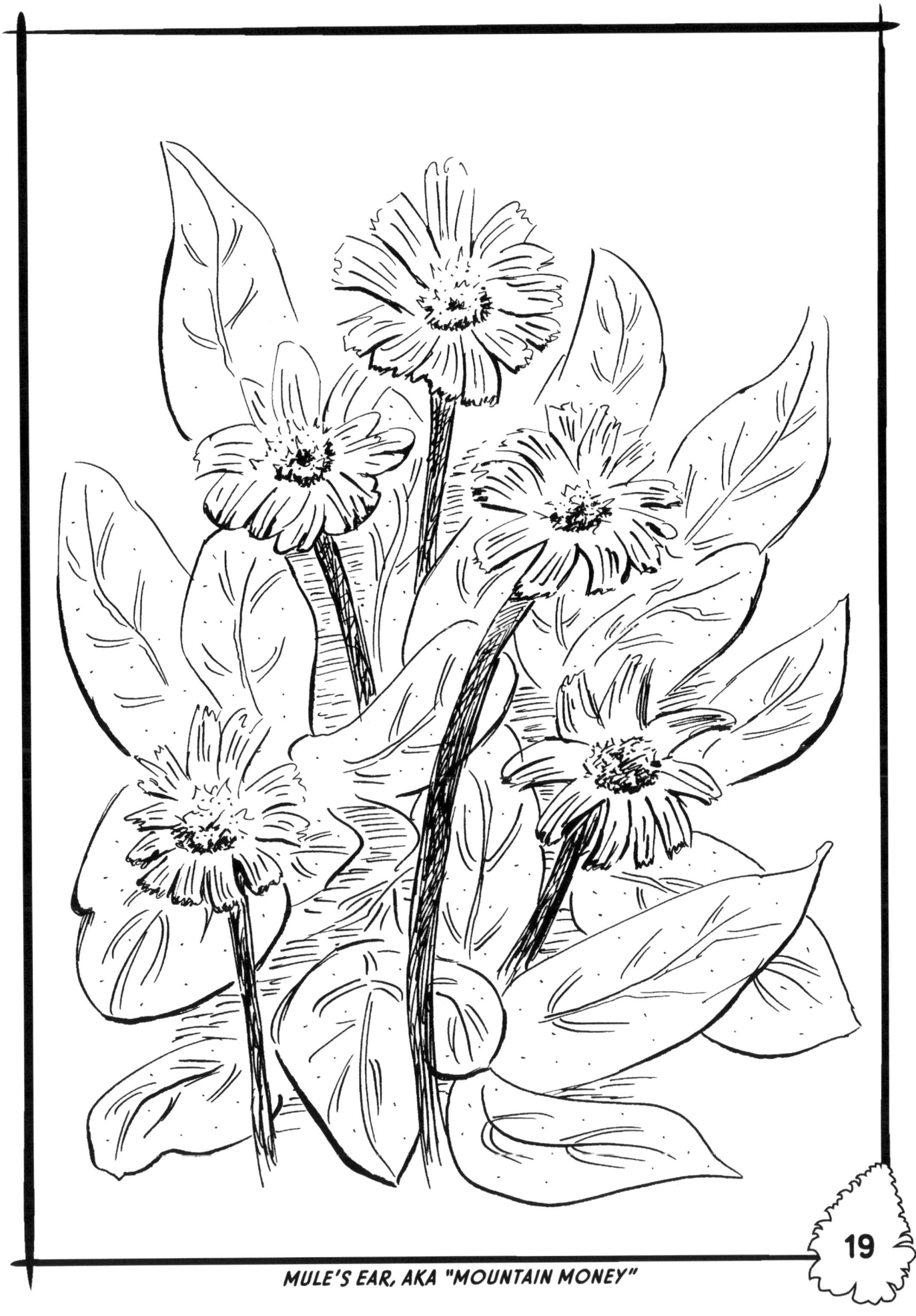

MULE'S EAR, AKA "MOUNTAIN MONEY"

19

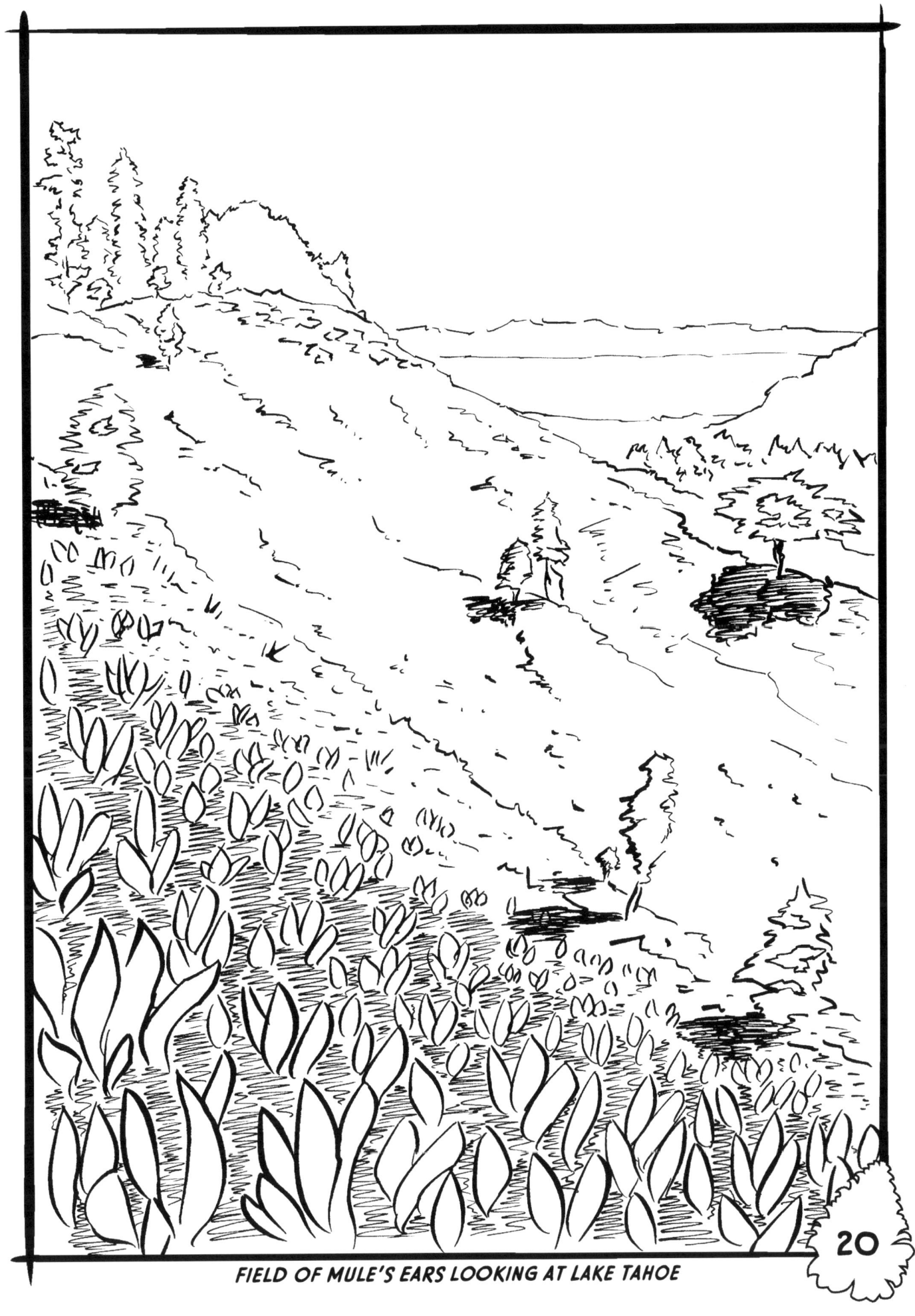

20

FIELD OF MULE'S EARS LOOKING AT LAKE TAHOE

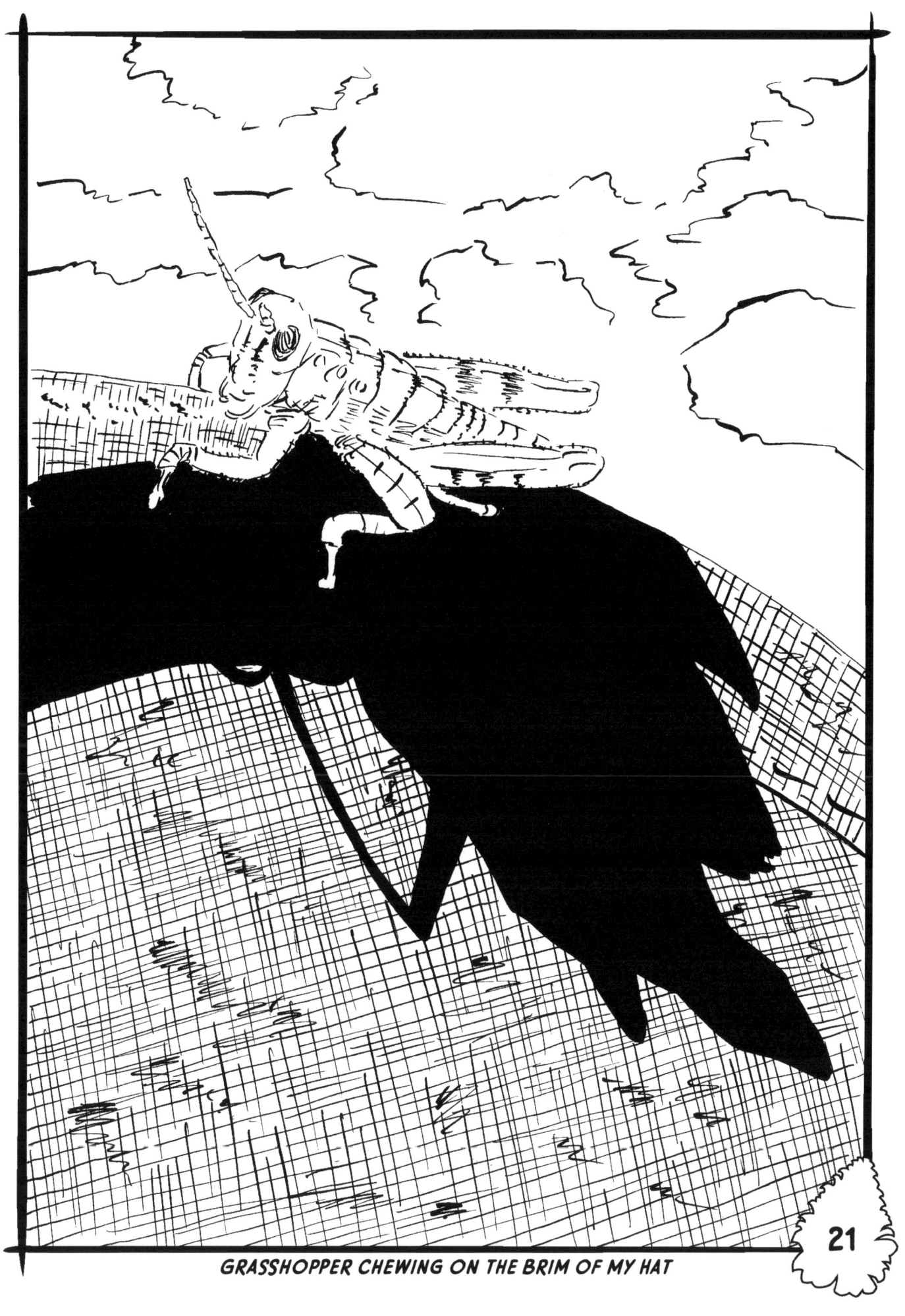

GRASSHOPPER CHEWING ON THE BRIM OF MY HAT

21

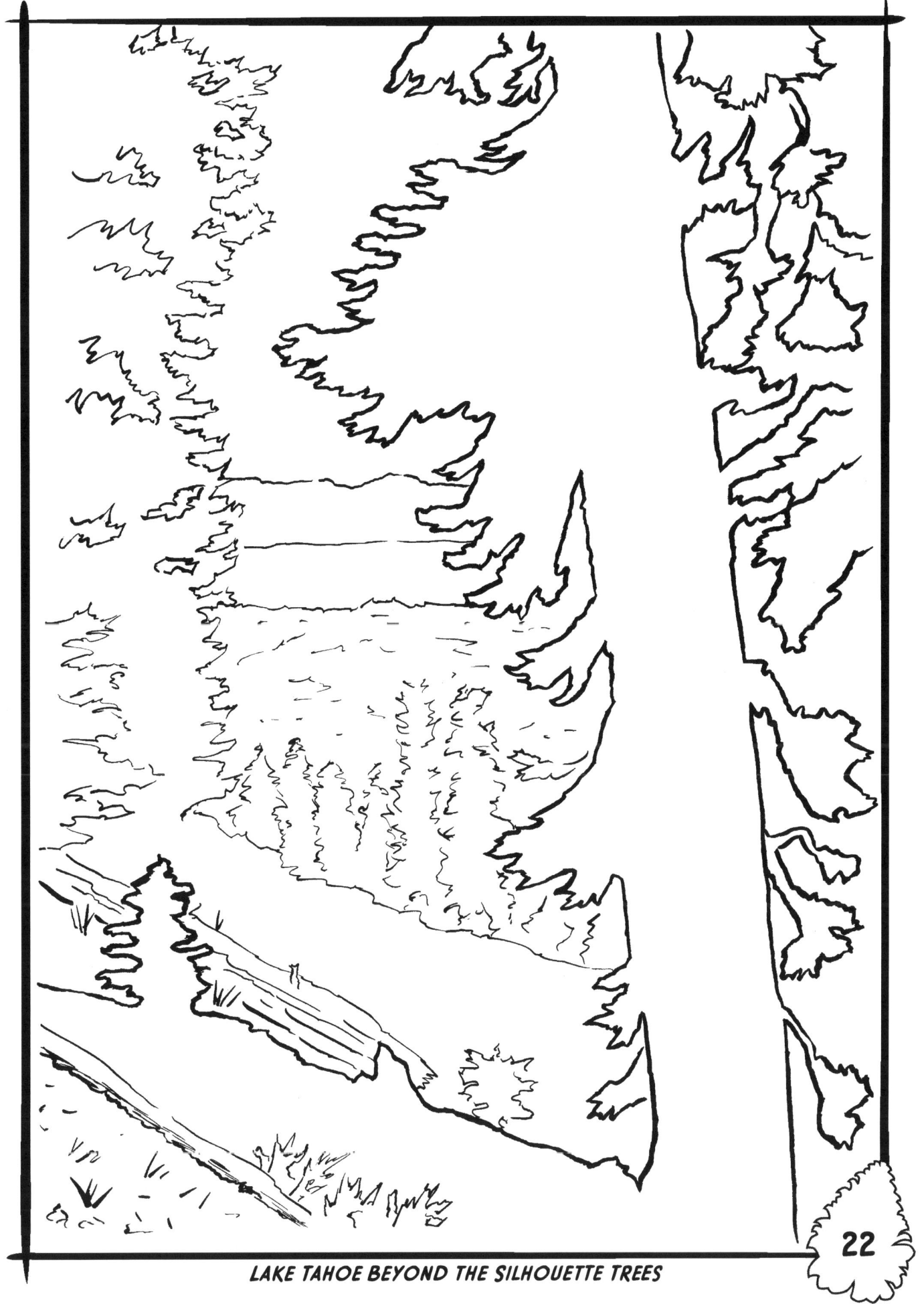

22

LAKE TAHOE BEYOND THE SILHOUETTE TREES

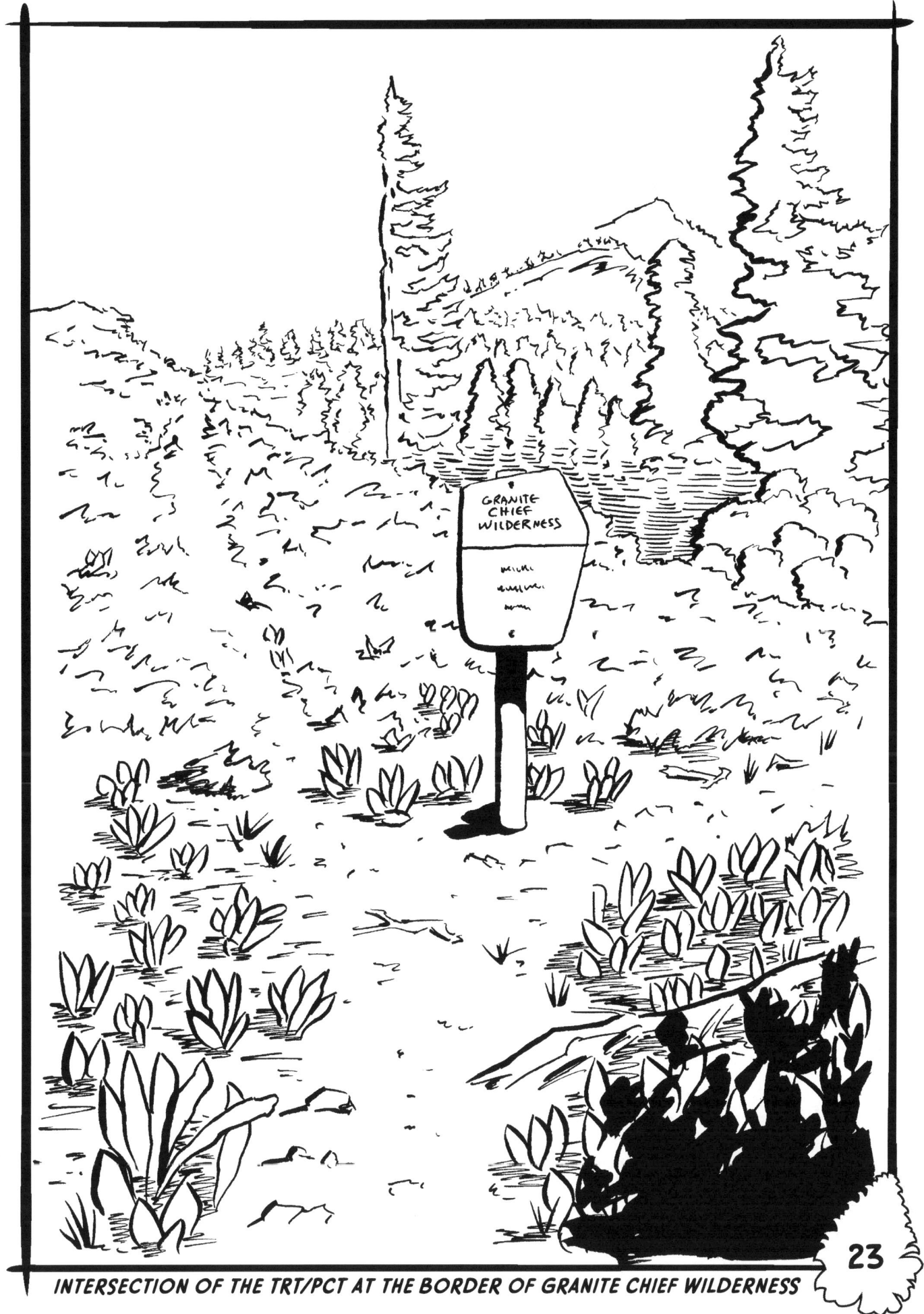

23

INTERSECTION OF THE TRT/PCT AT THE BORDER OF GRANITE CHIEF WILDERNESS

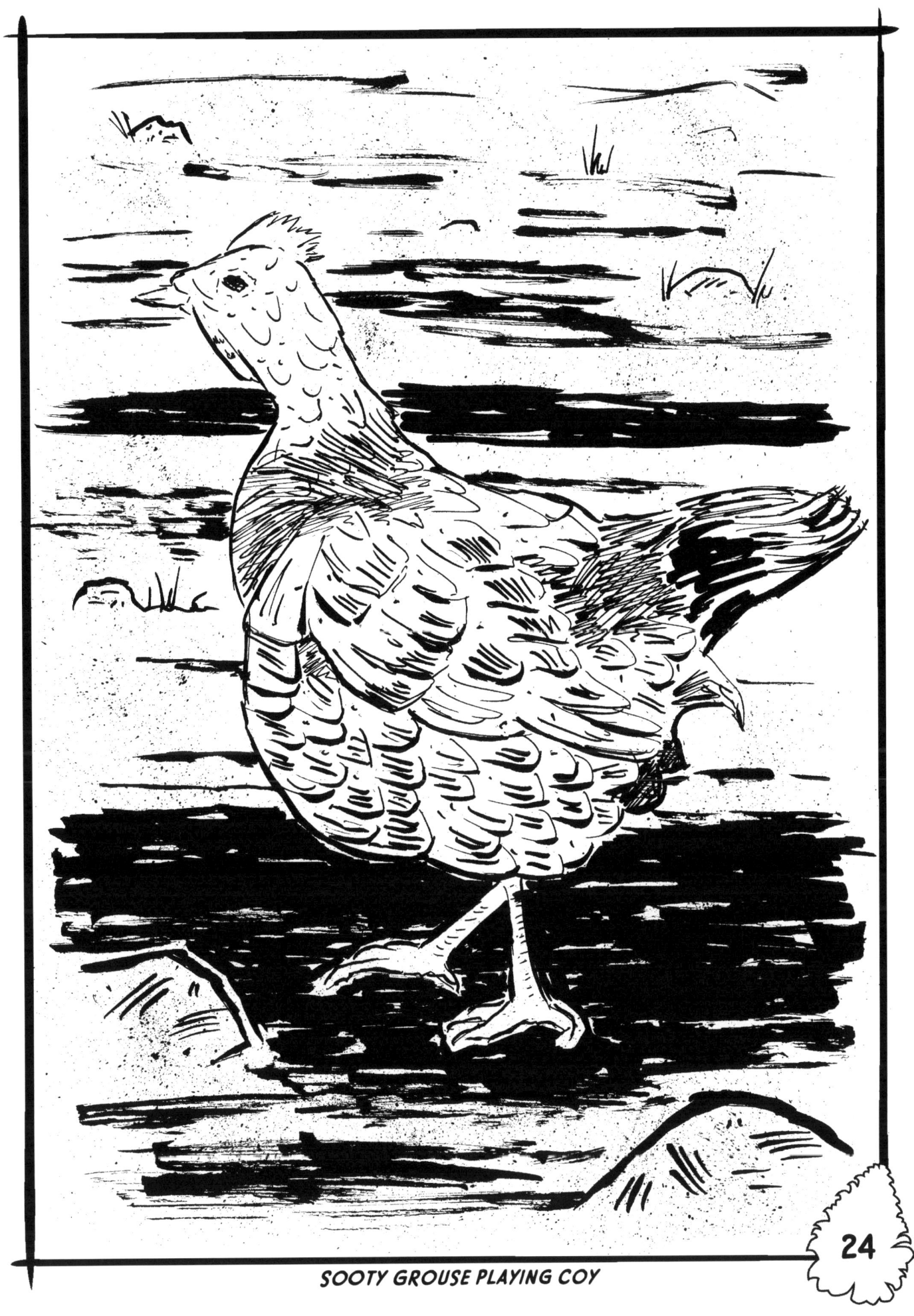

SOOTY GROUSE PLAYING COY

24

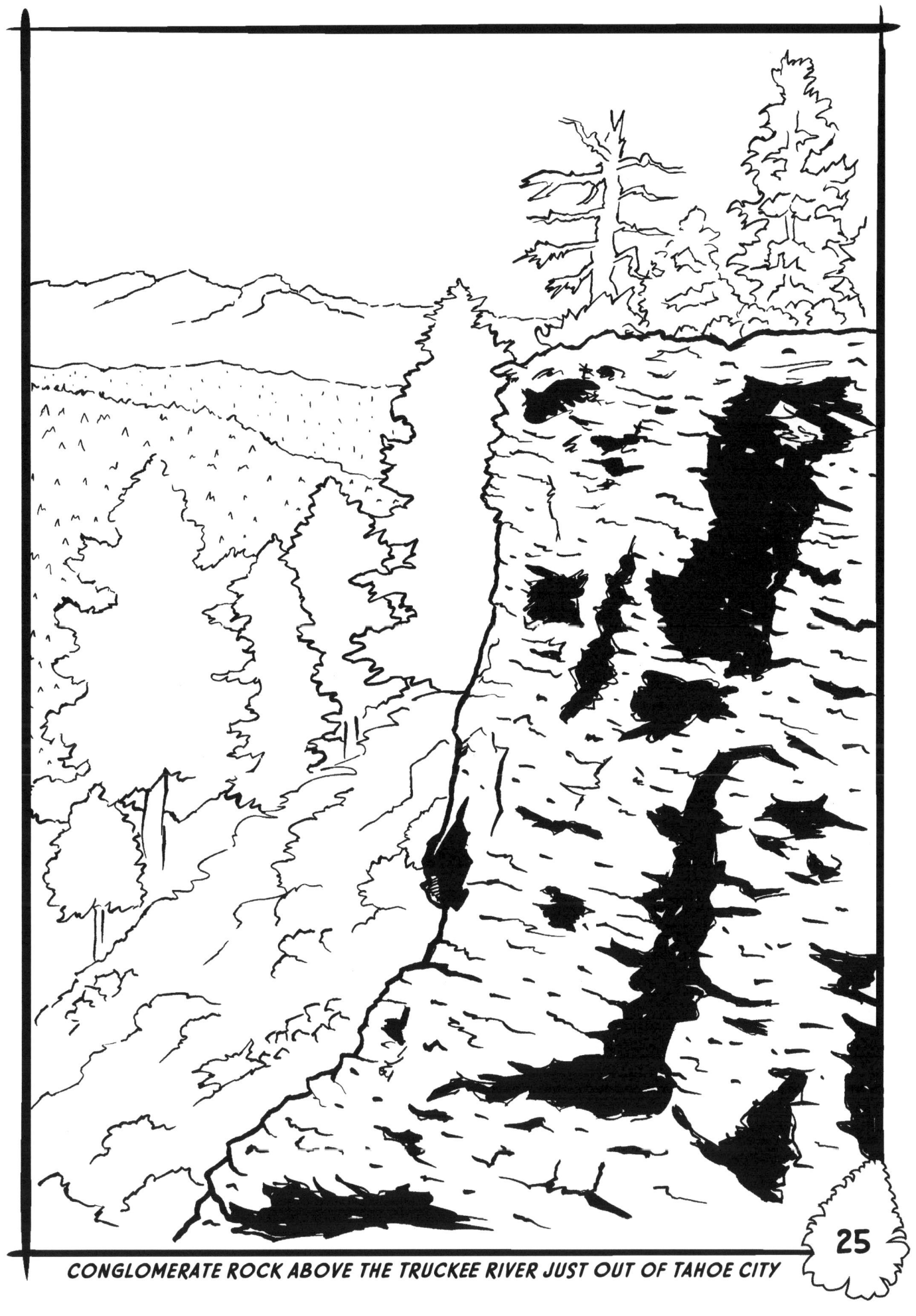

25

CONGLOMERATE ROCK ABOVE THE TRUCKEE RIVER JUST OUT OF TAHOE CITY

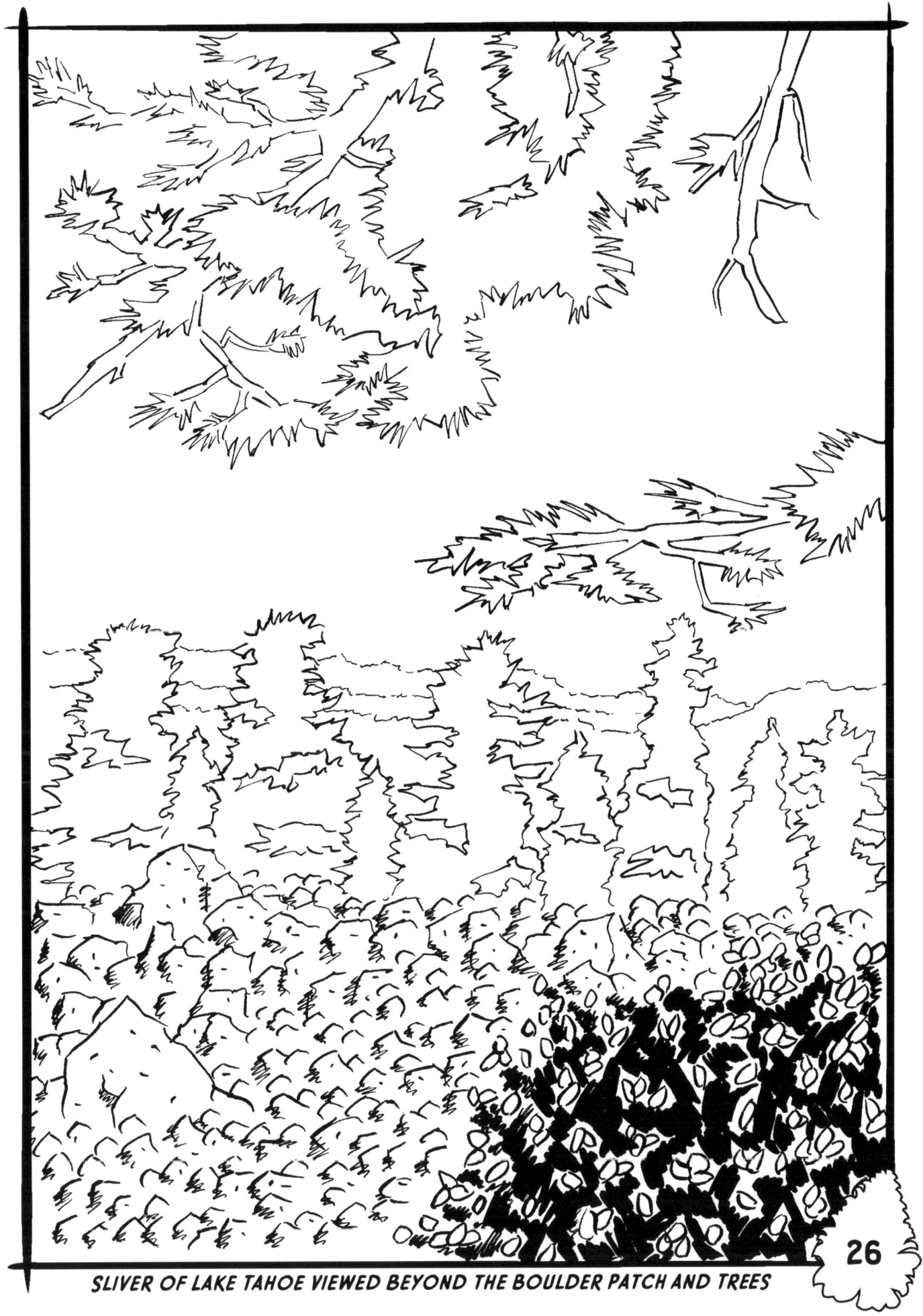

26

SLIVER OF LAKE TAHOE VIEWED BEYOND THE BOULDER PATCH AND TREES

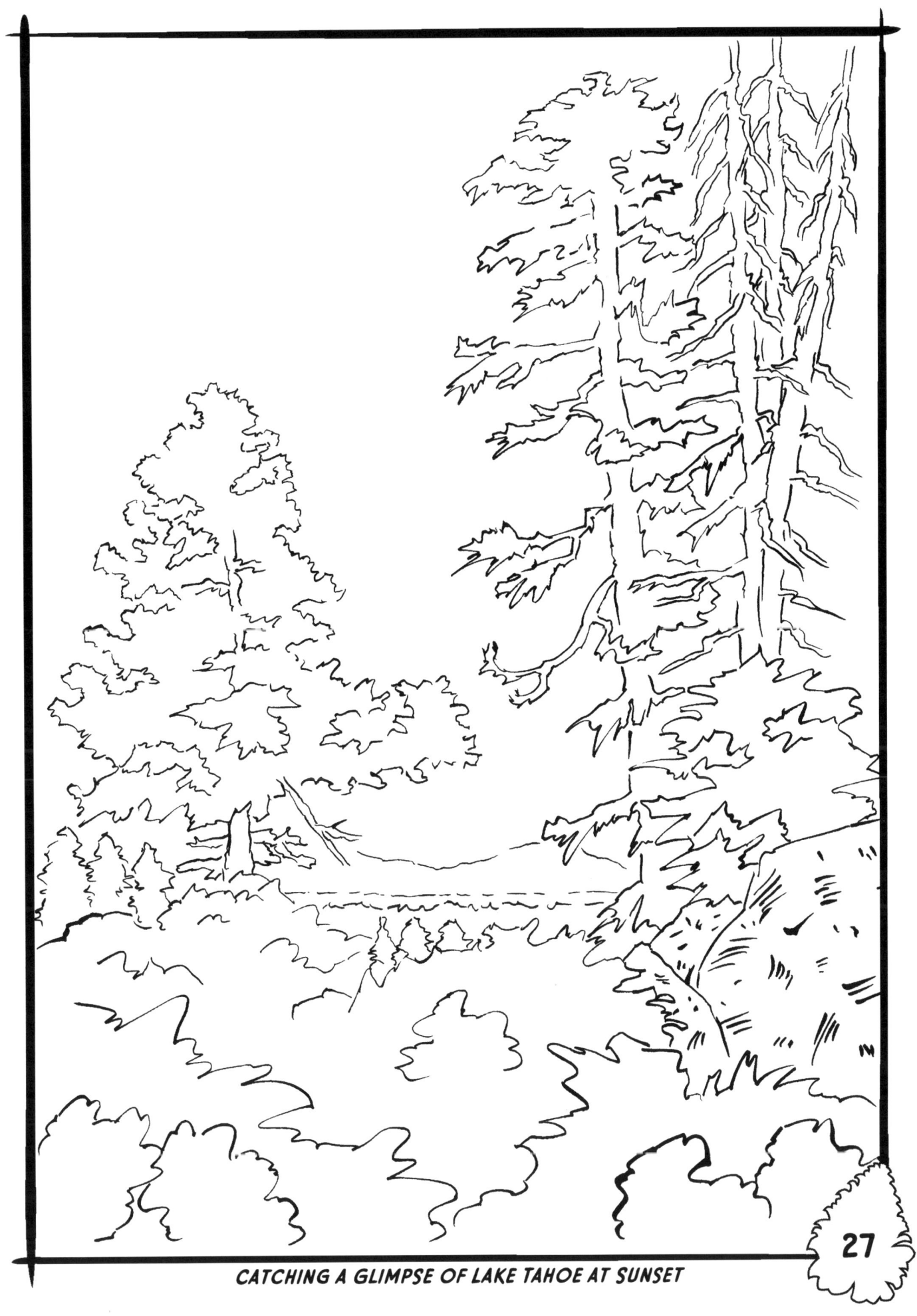

27

CATCHING A GLIMPSE OF LAKE TAHOE AT SUNSET

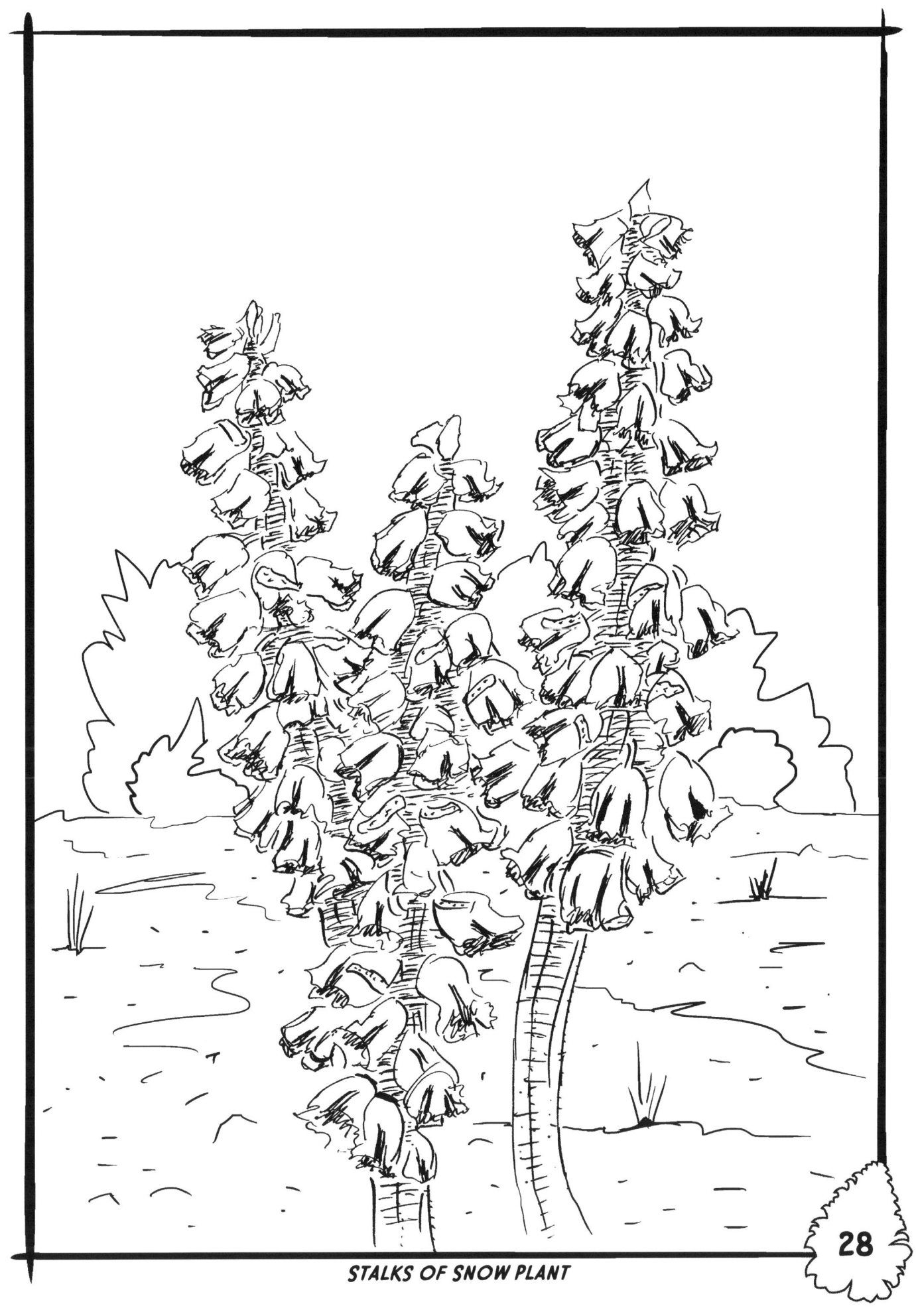

STALKS OF SNOW PLANT

28

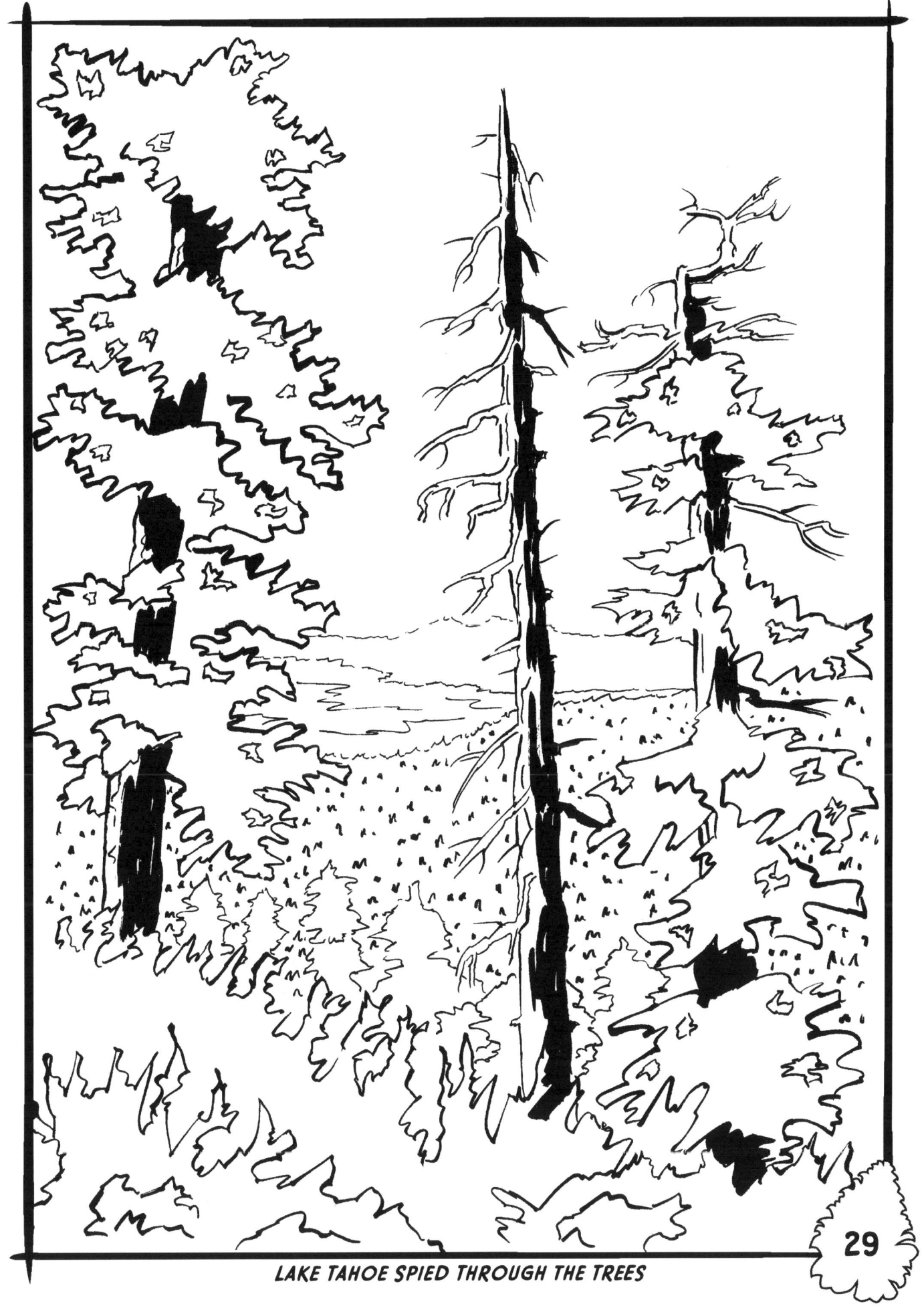

LAKE TAHOE SPIED THROUGH THE TREES

29

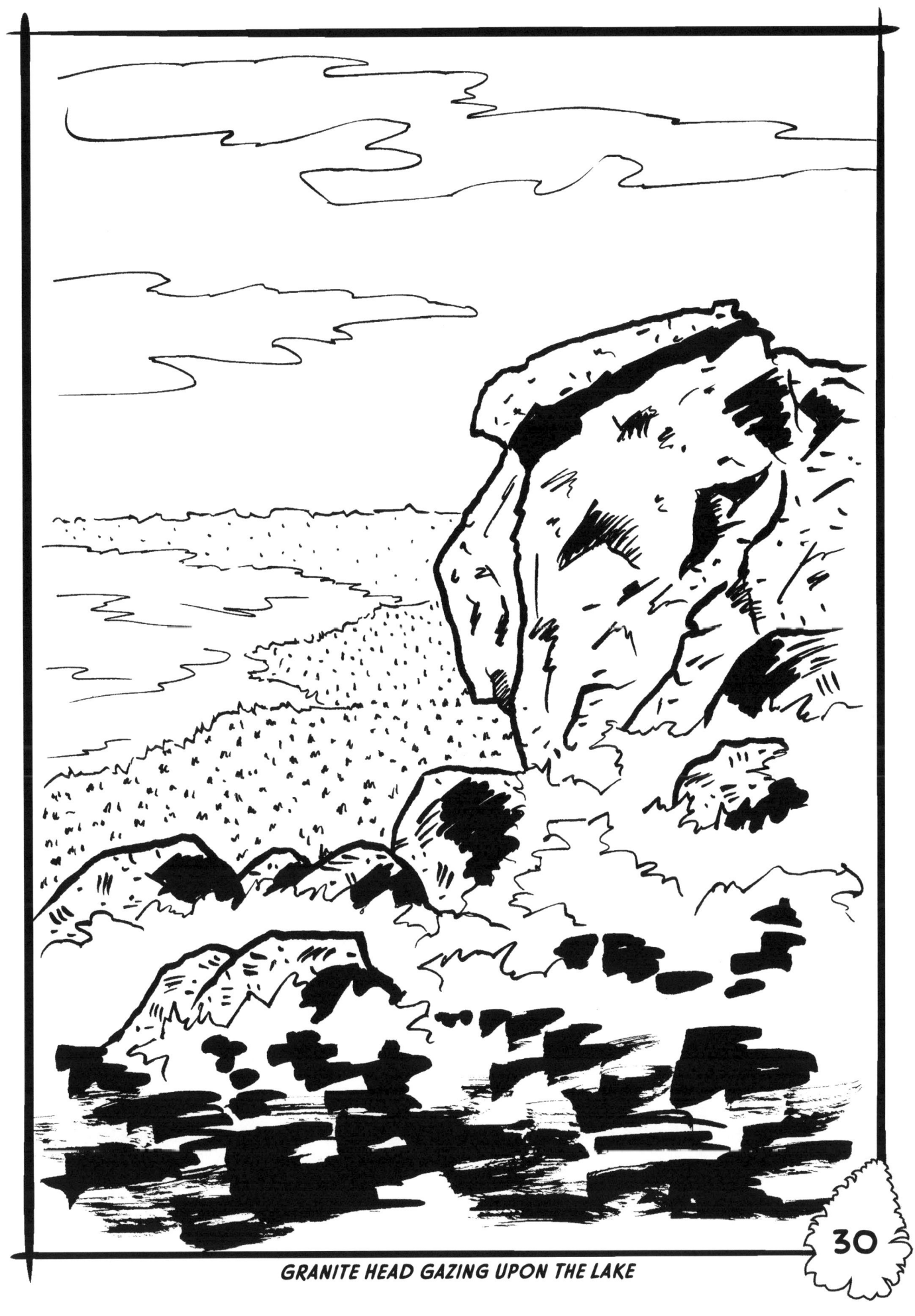

GRANITE HEAD GAZING UPON THE LAKE

30

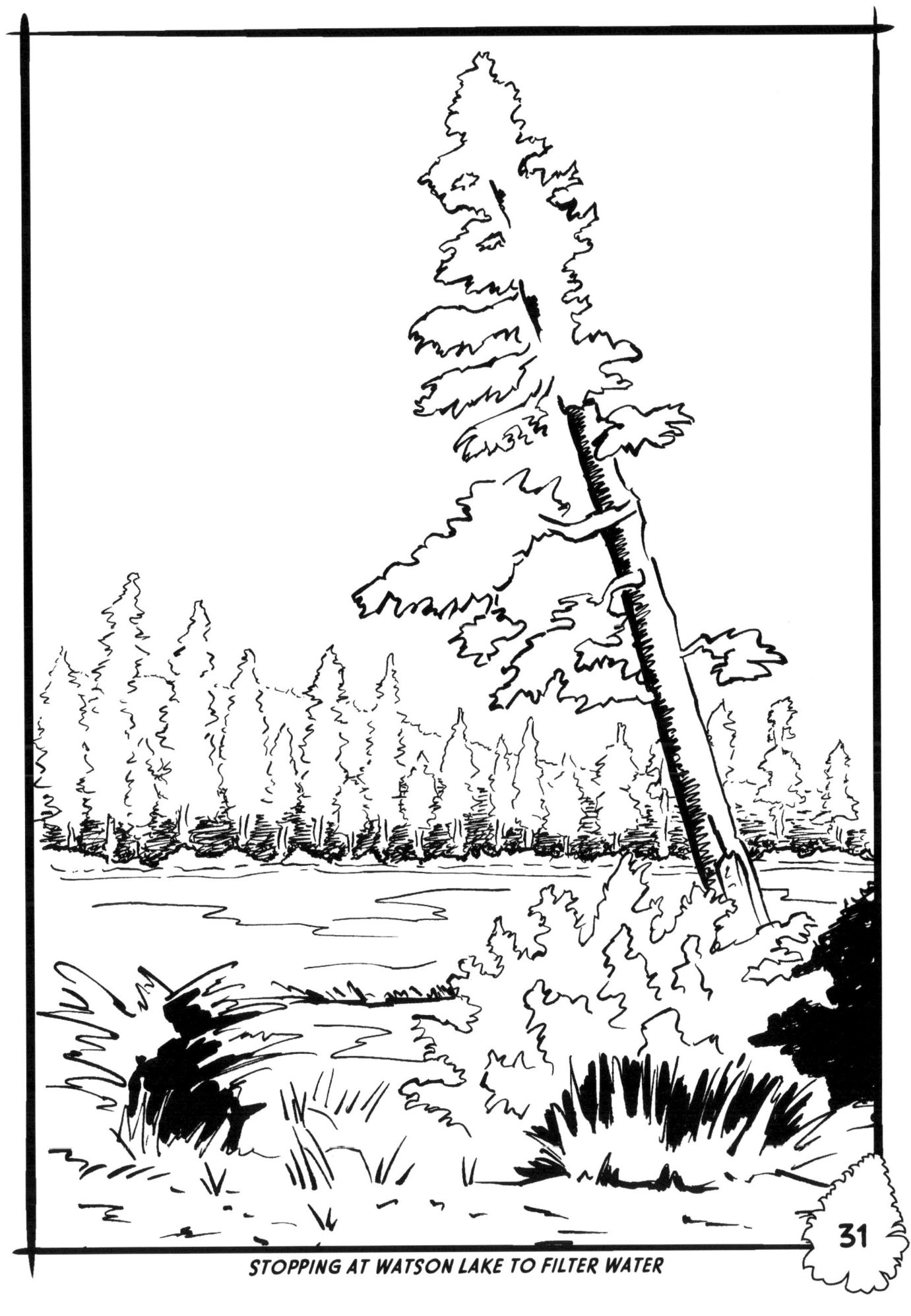

31

STOPPING AT WATSON LAKE TO FILTER WATER

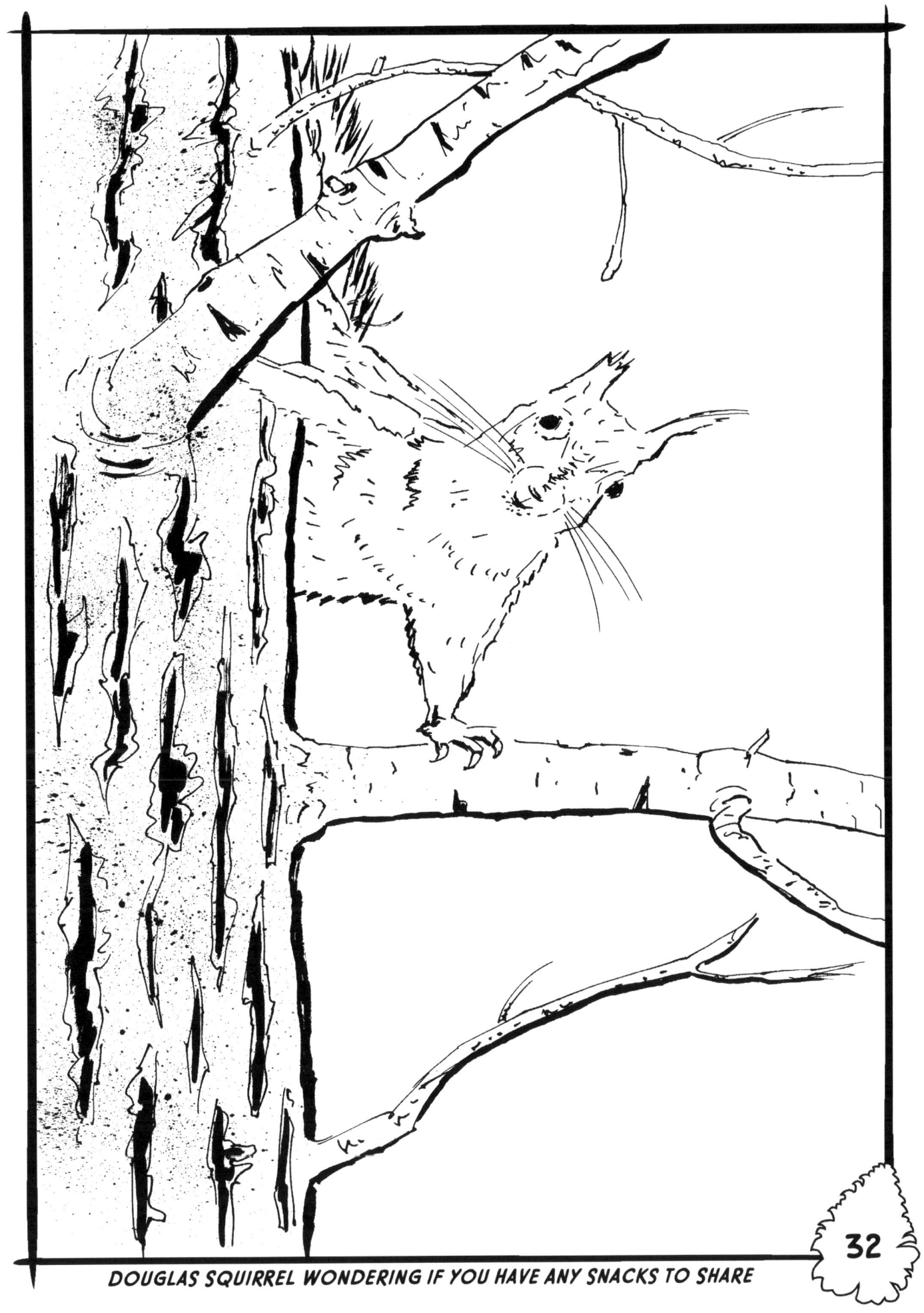

DOUGLAS SQUIRREL WONDERING IF YOU HAVE ANY SNACKS TO SHARE

32

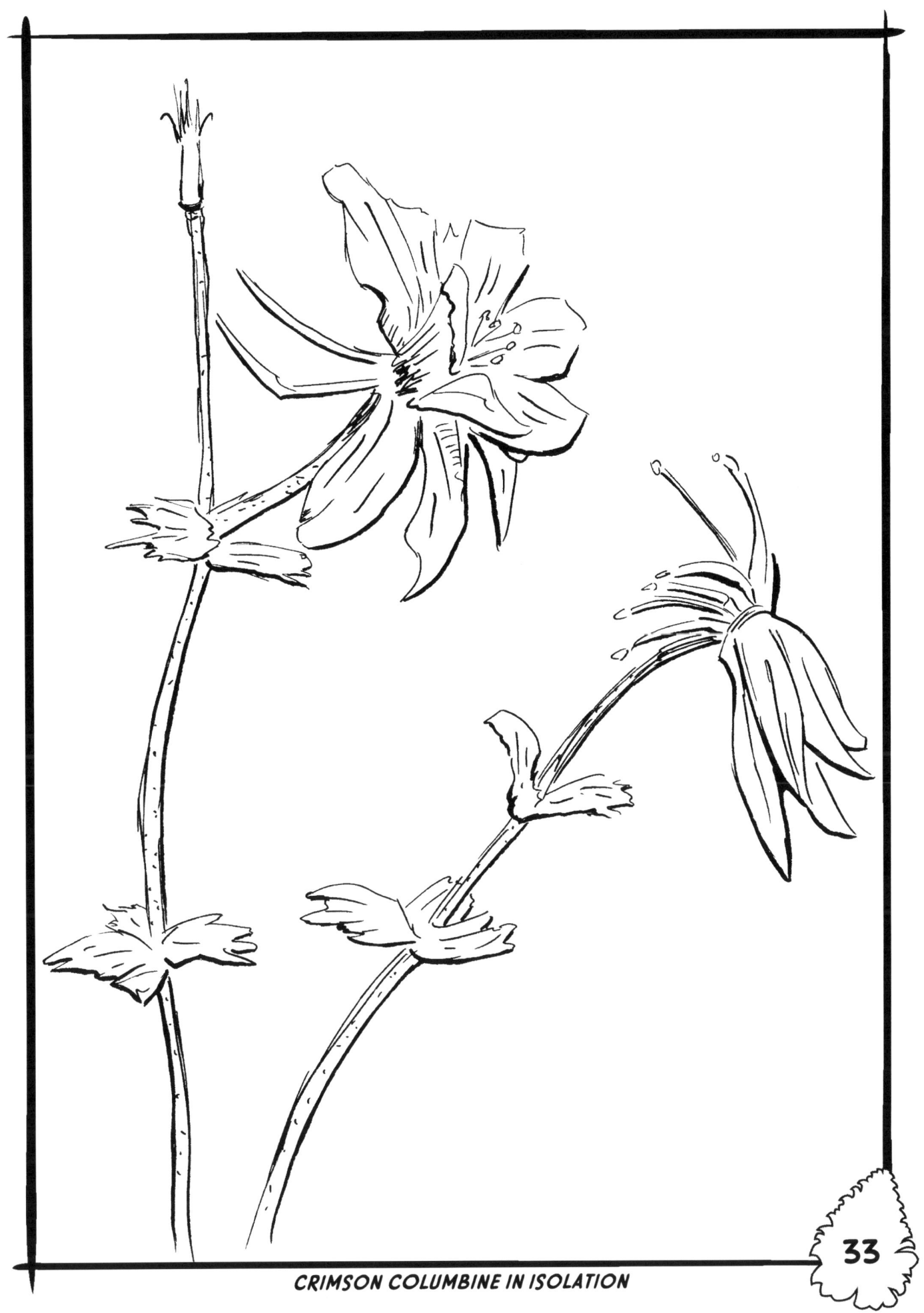

CRIMSON COLUMBINE IN ISOLATION

33

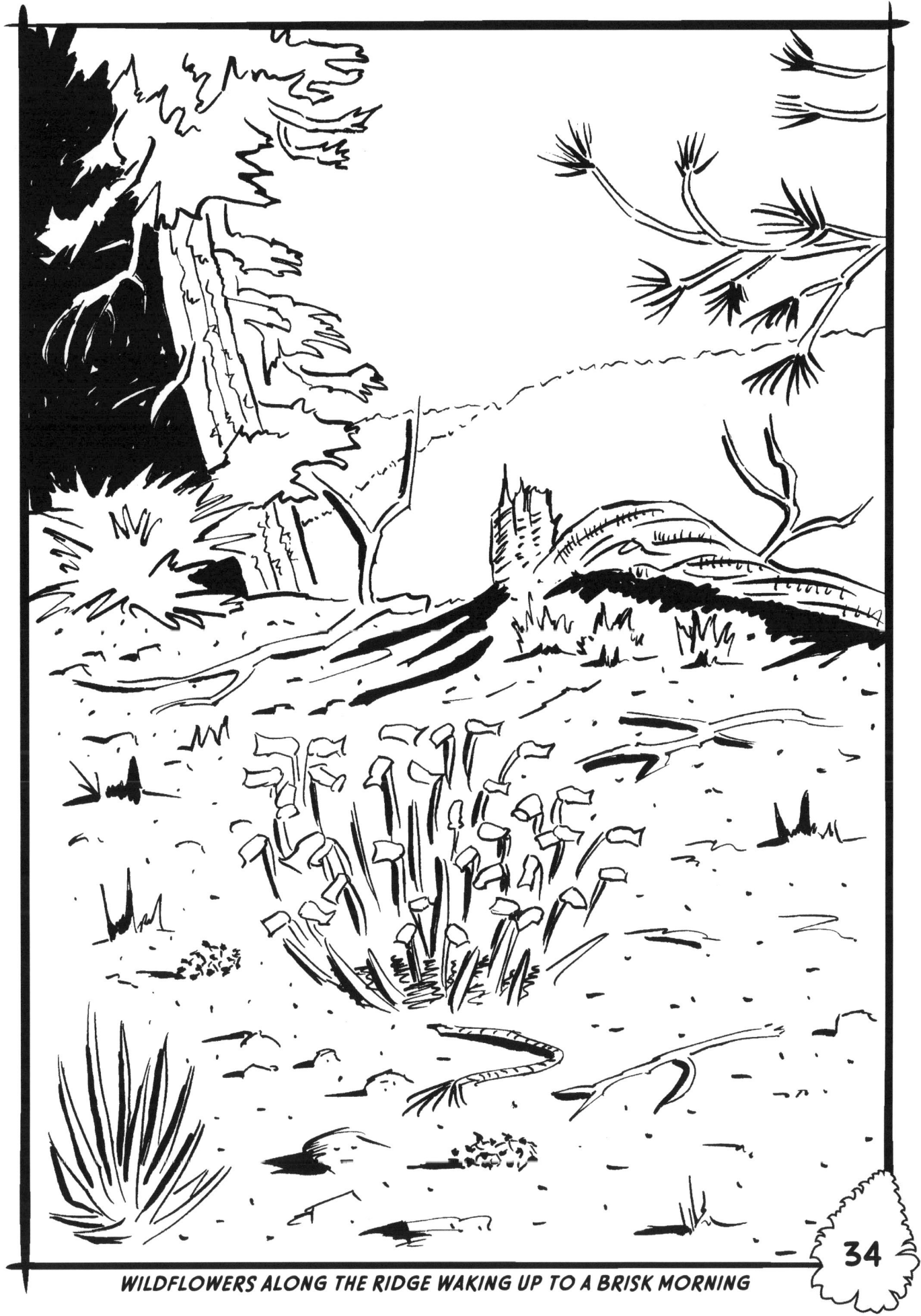

WILDFLOWERS ALONG THE RIDGE WAKING UP TO A BRISK MORNING

34

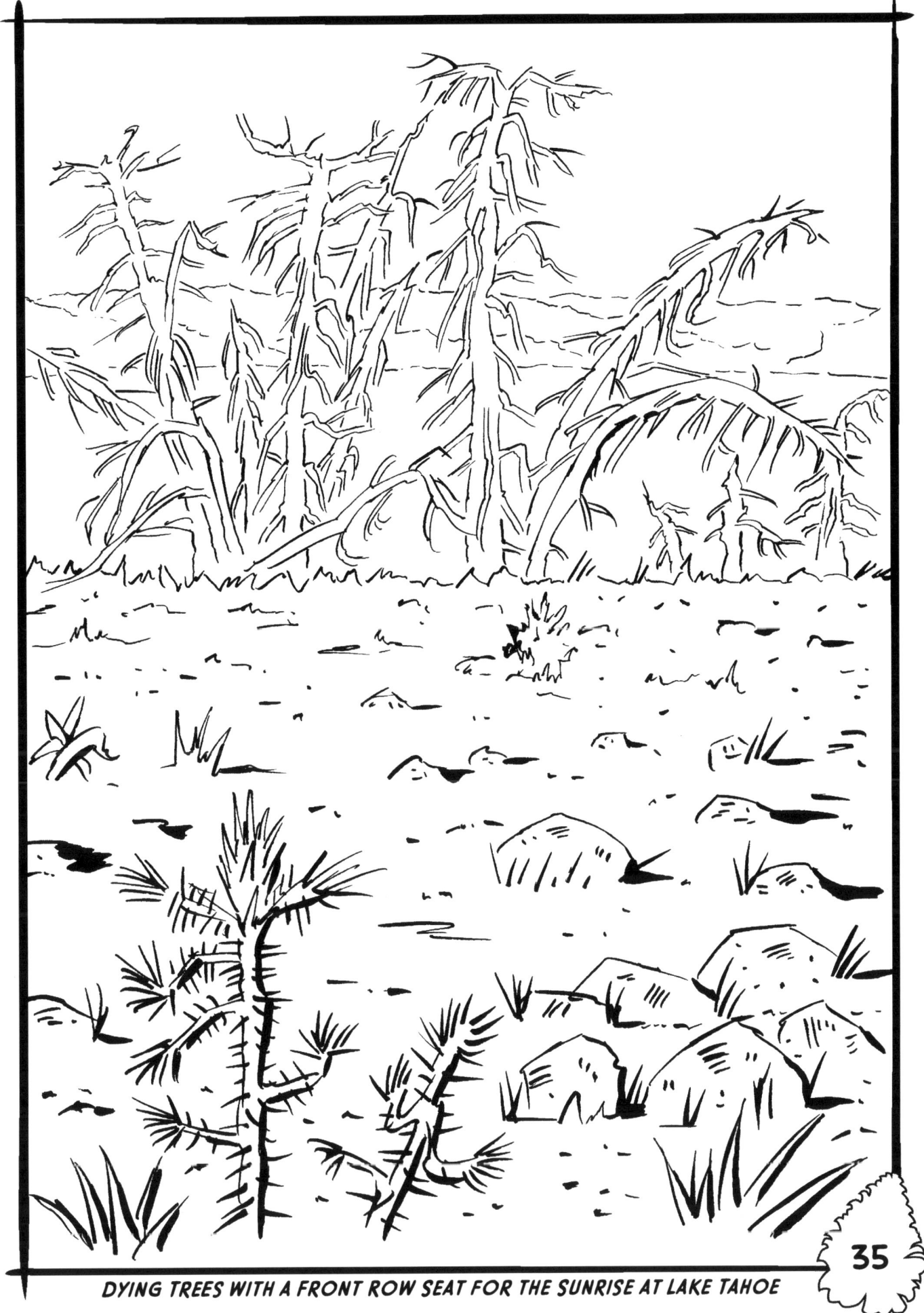

DYING TREES WITH A FRONT ROW SEAT FOR THE SUNRISE AT LAKE TAHOE

35

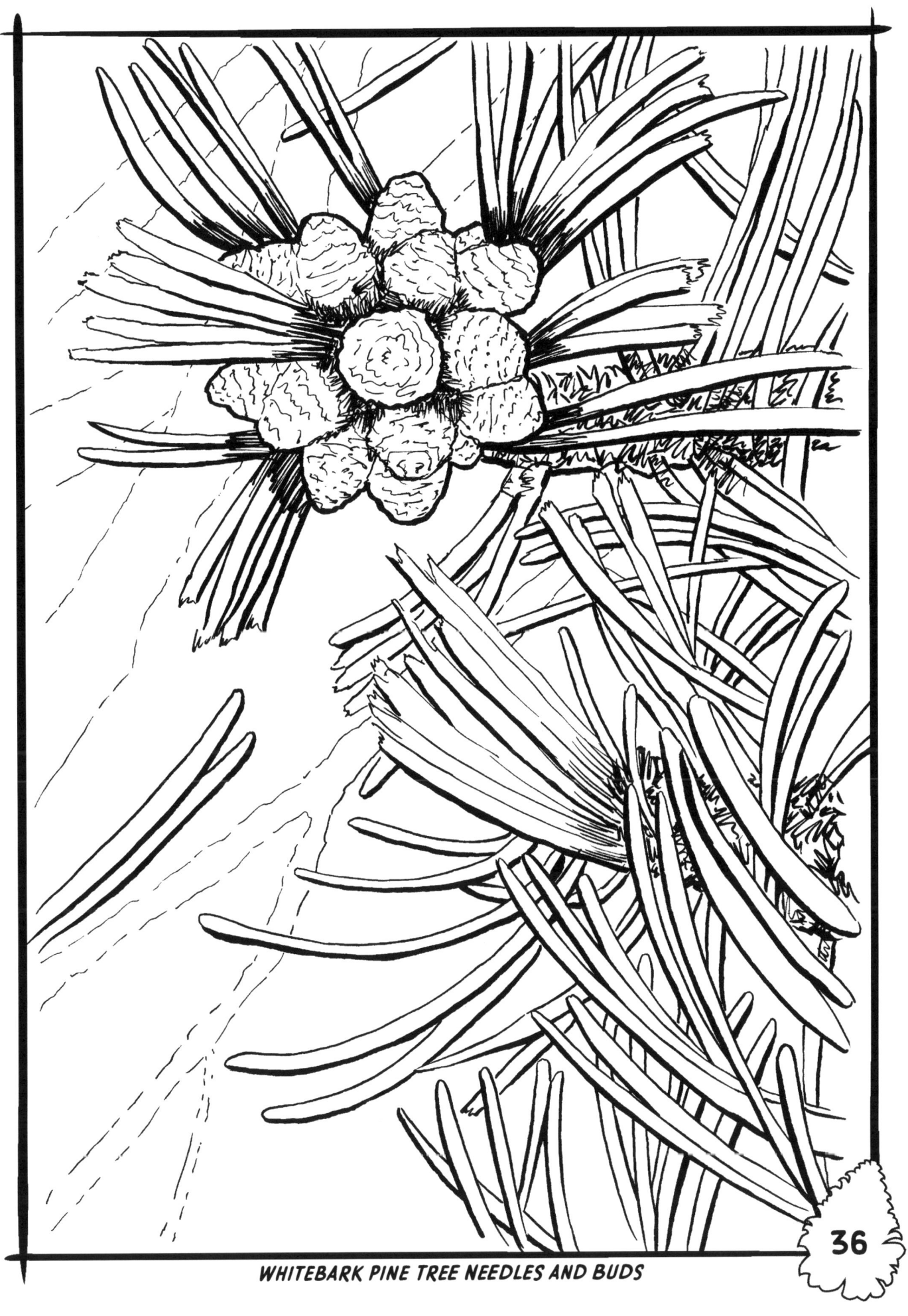

36

WHITEBARK PINE TREE NEEDLES AND BUDS

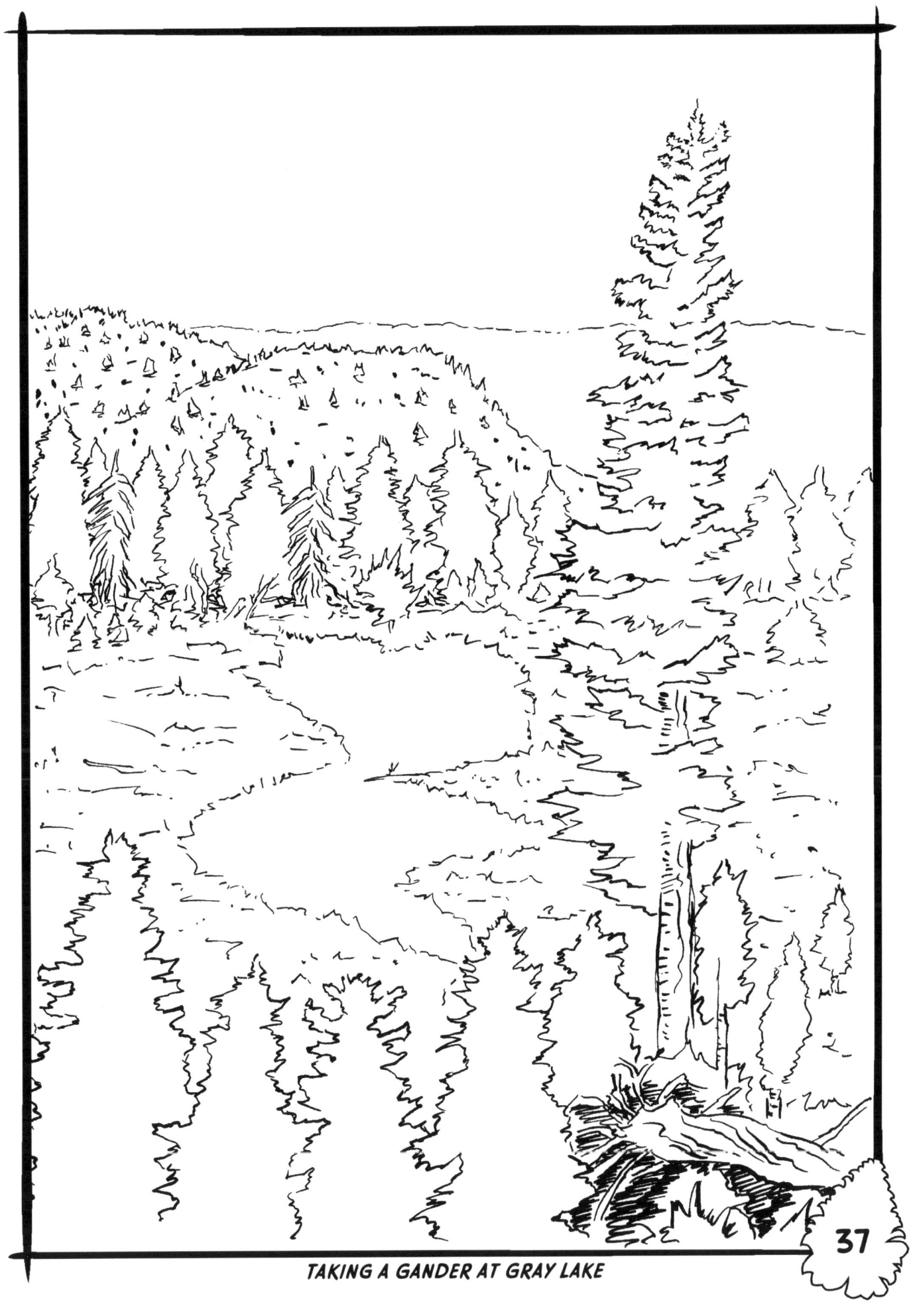

37

TAKING A GANDER AT GRAY LAKE

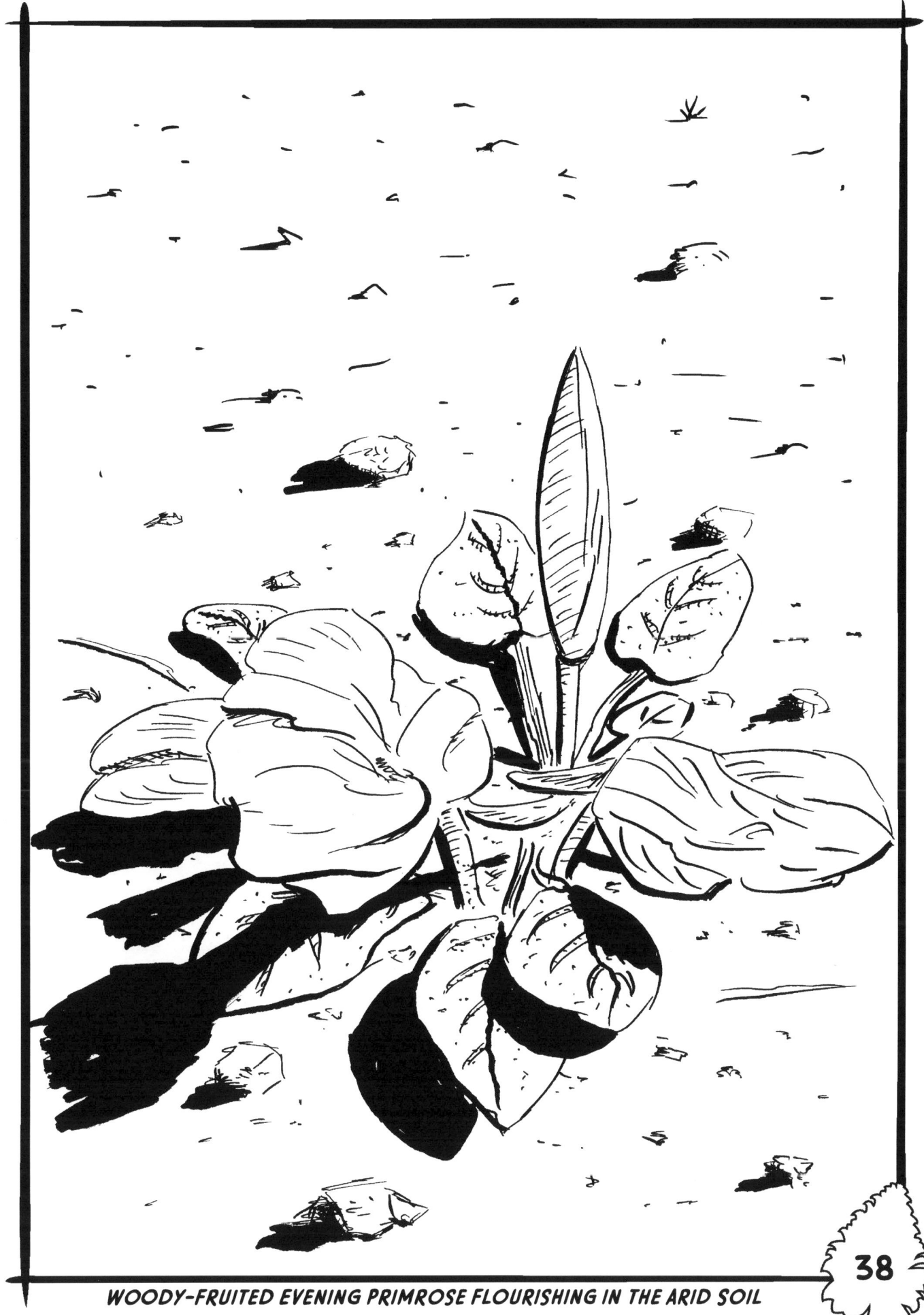

WOODY-FRUITED EVENING PRIMROSE FLOURISHING IN THE ARID SOIL

38

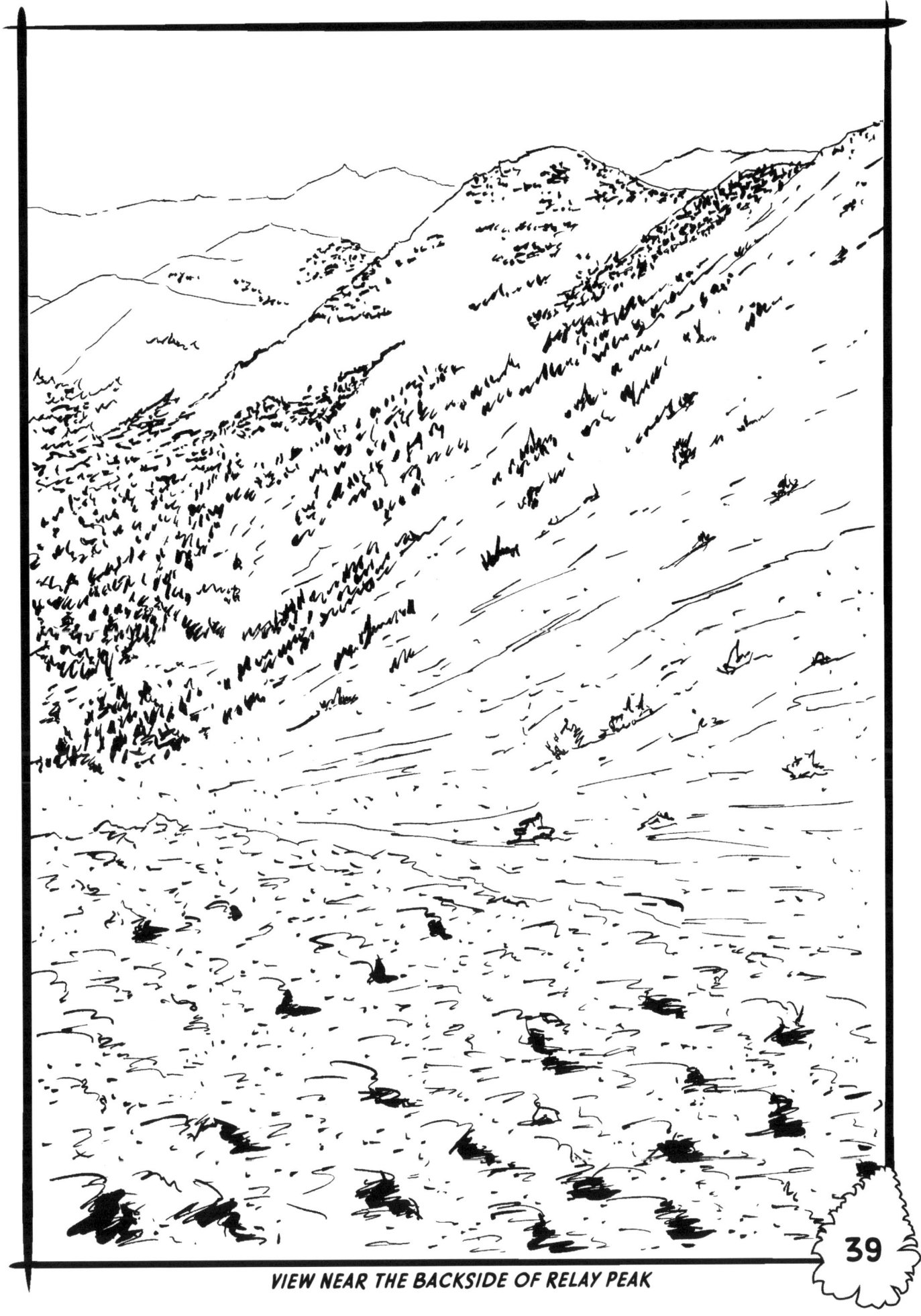

39

VIEW NEAR THE BACKSIDE OF RELAY PEAK

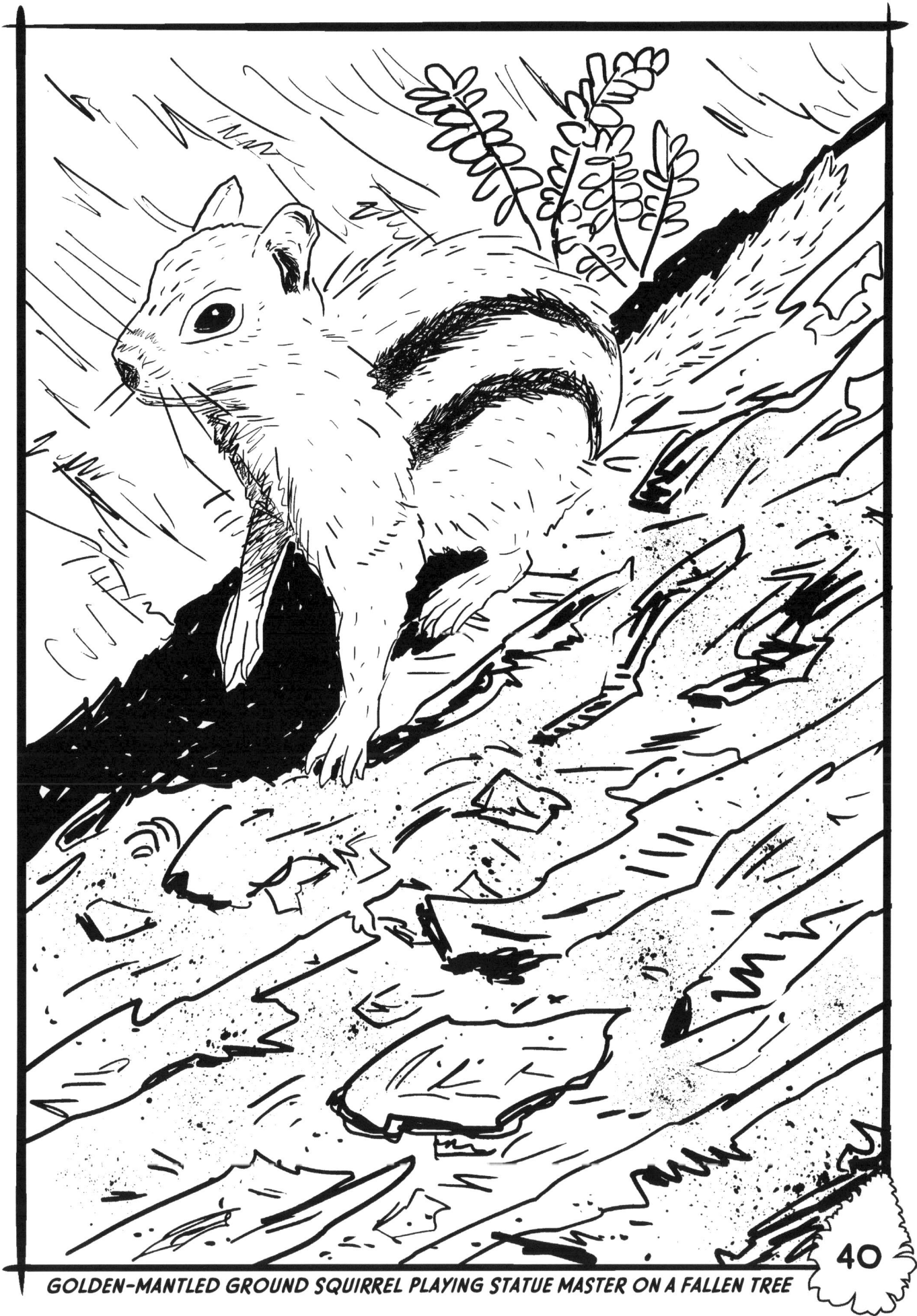

GOLDEN-MANTLED GROUND SQUIRREL PLAYING STATUE MASTER ON A FALLEN TREE

40

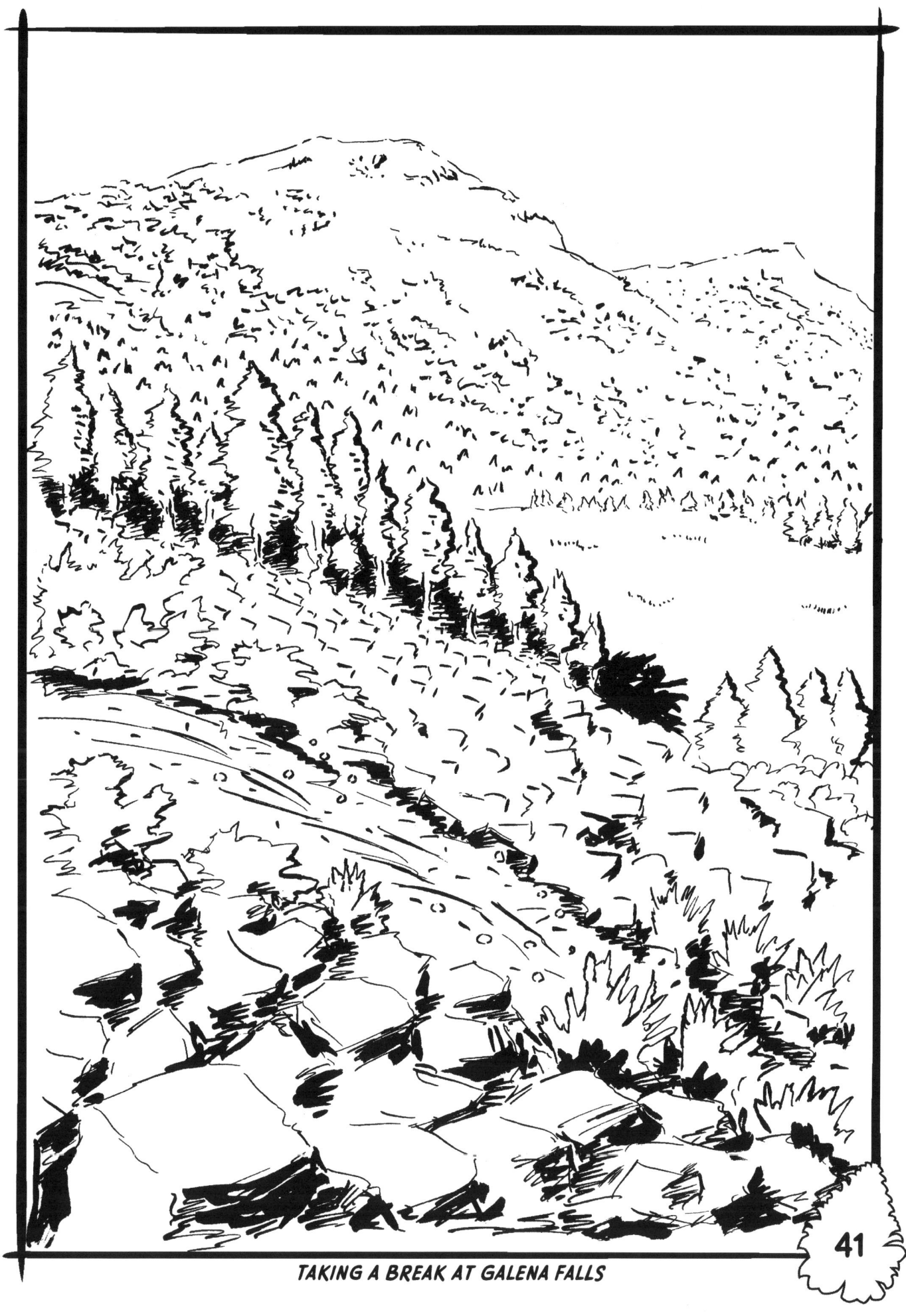

41

TAKING A BREAK AT GALENA FALLS

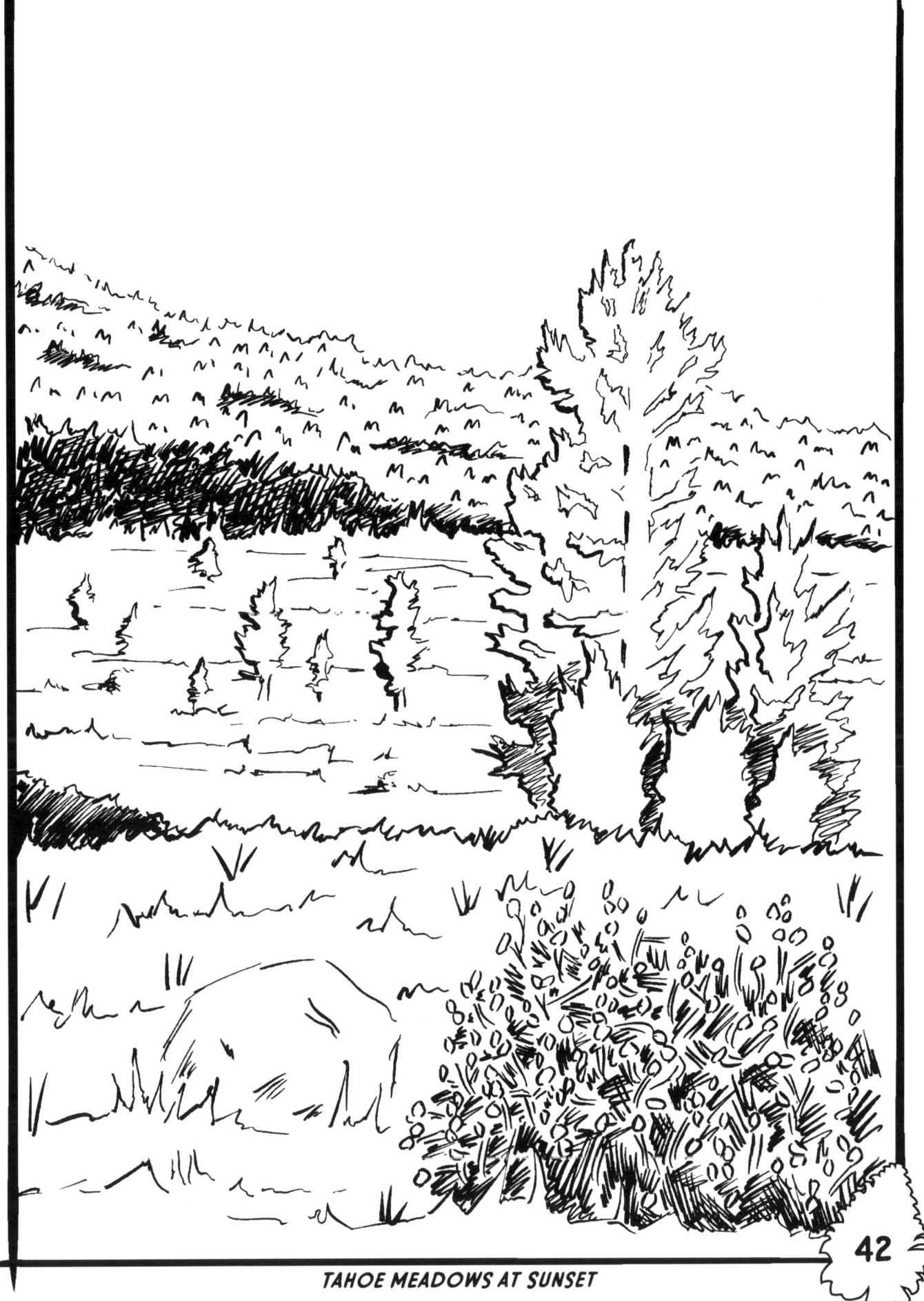

42

TAHOE MEADOWS AT SUNSET

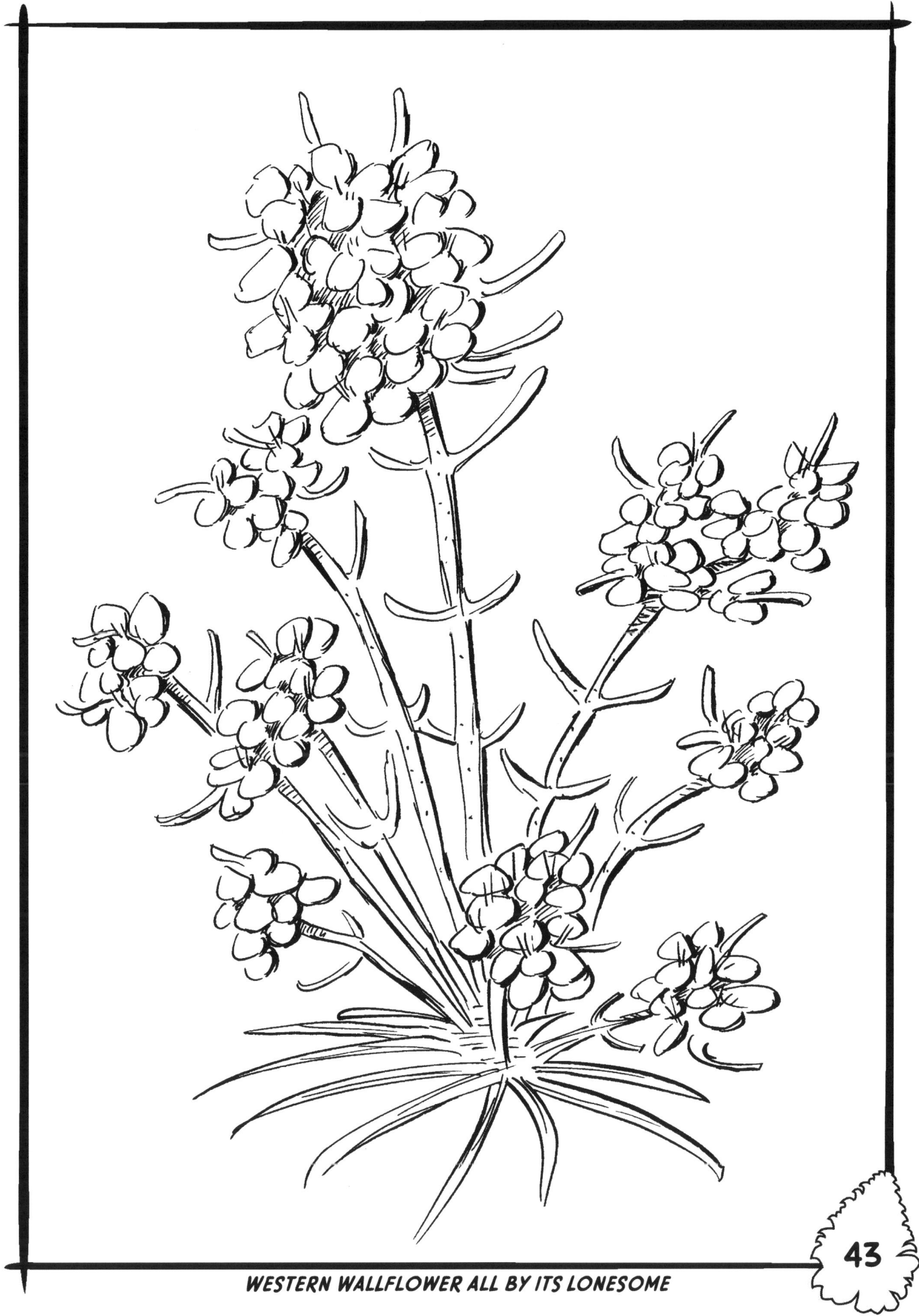

43

WESTERN WALLFLOWER ALL BY ITS LONESOME

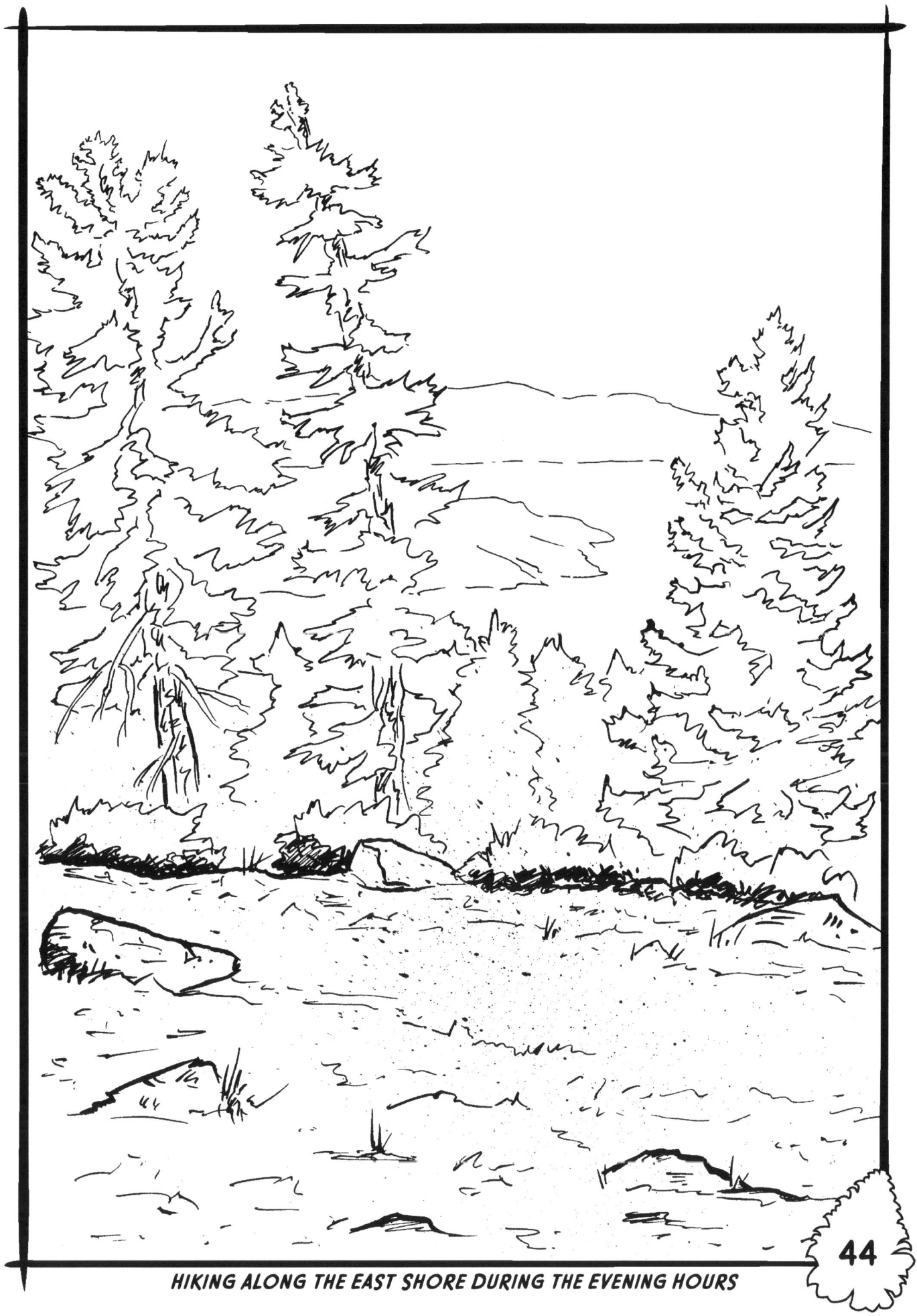

44

HIKING ALONG THE EAST SHORE DURING THE EVENING HOURS

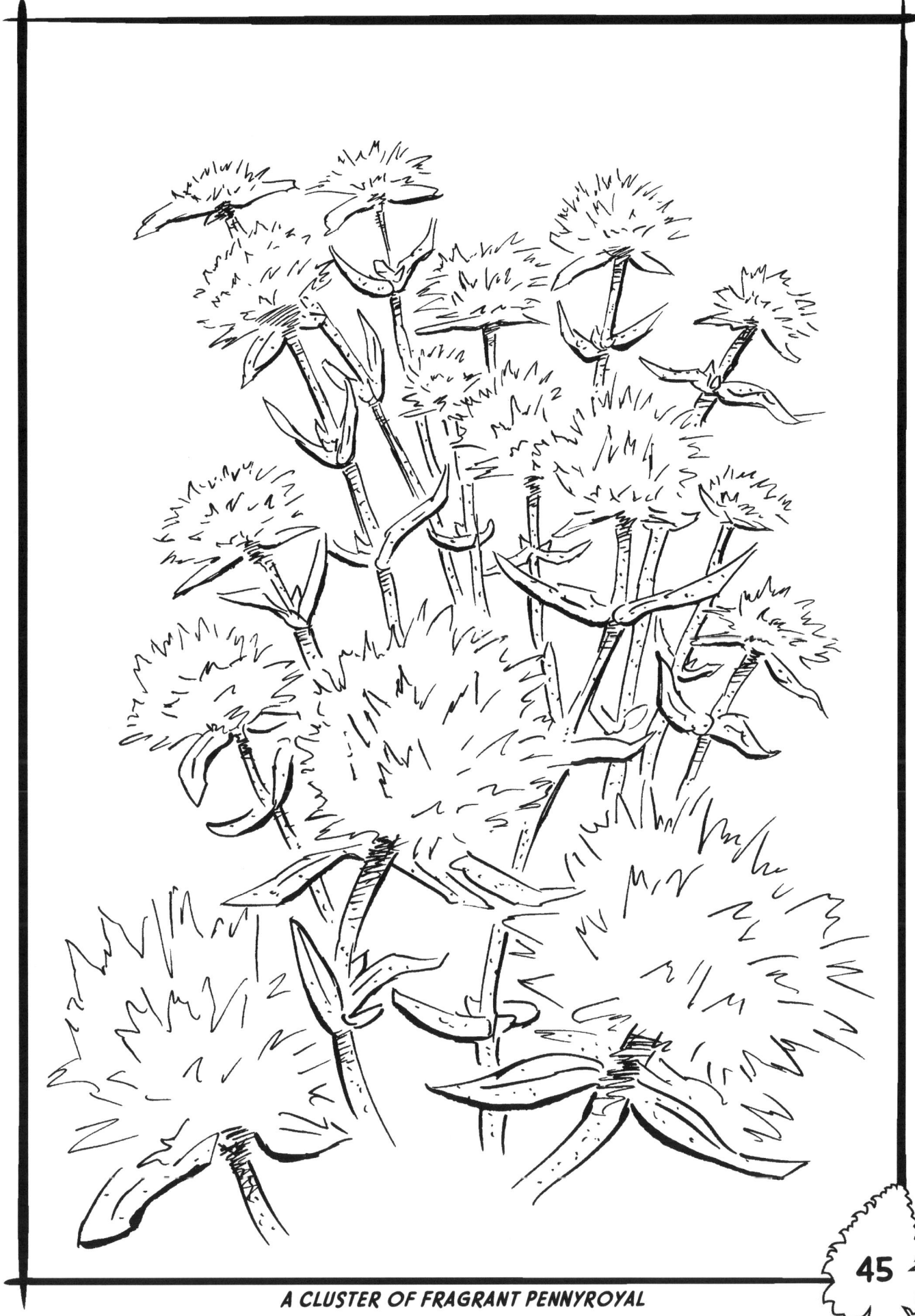

A CLUSTER OF FRAGRANT PENNYROYAL

45

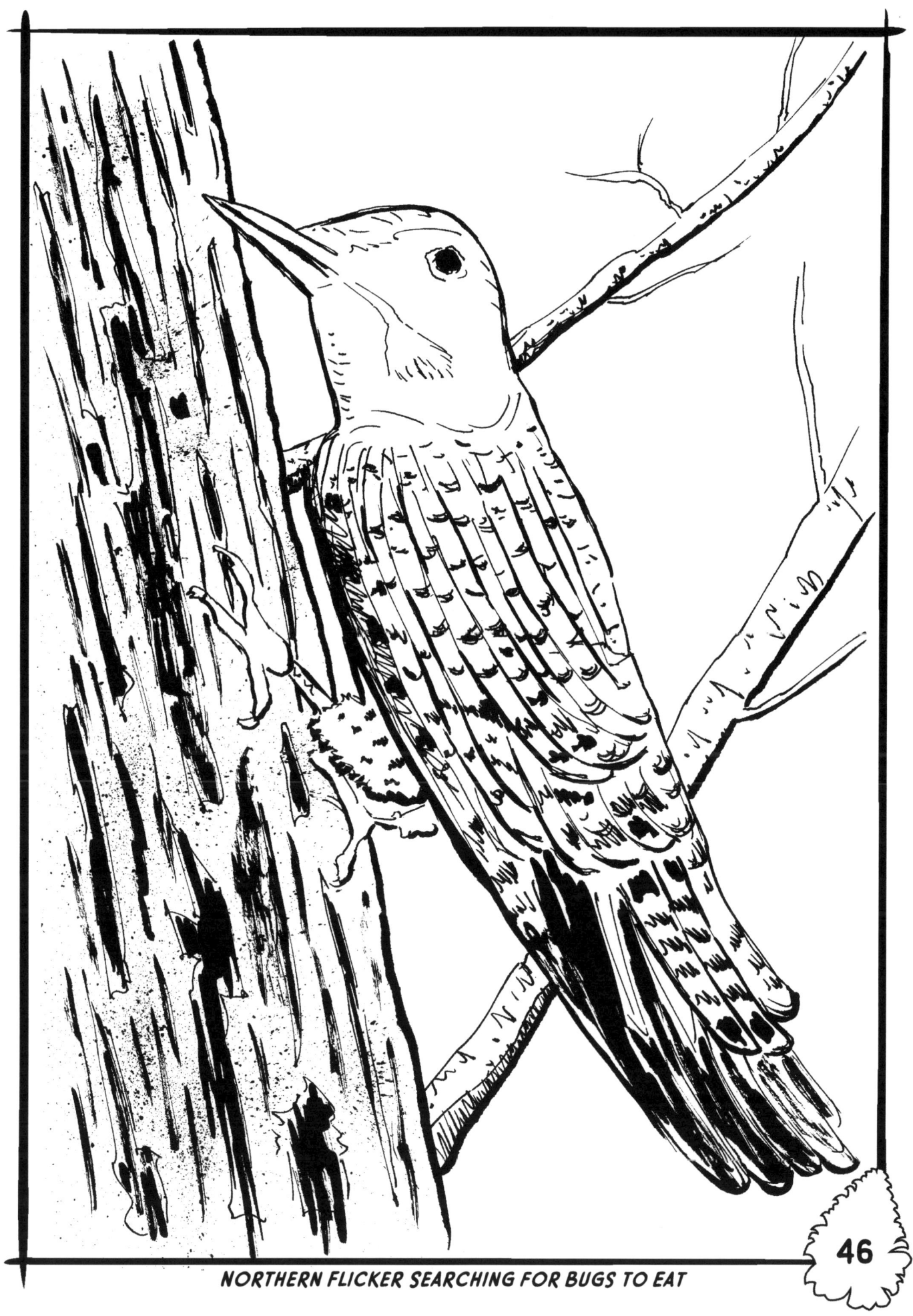

46

NORTHERN FLICKER SEARCHING FOR BUGS TO EAT

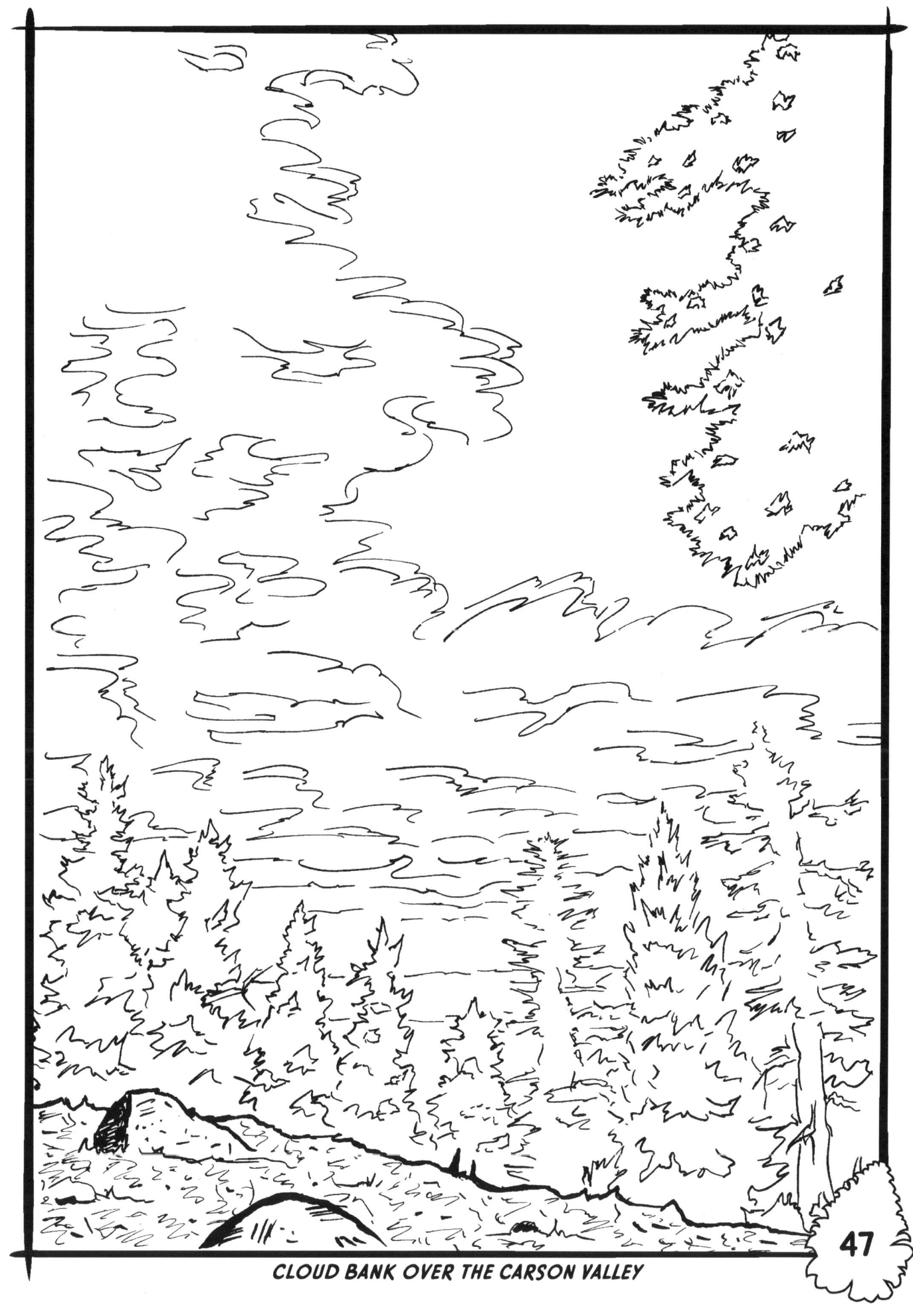

CLOUD BANK OVER THE CARSON VALLEY

47

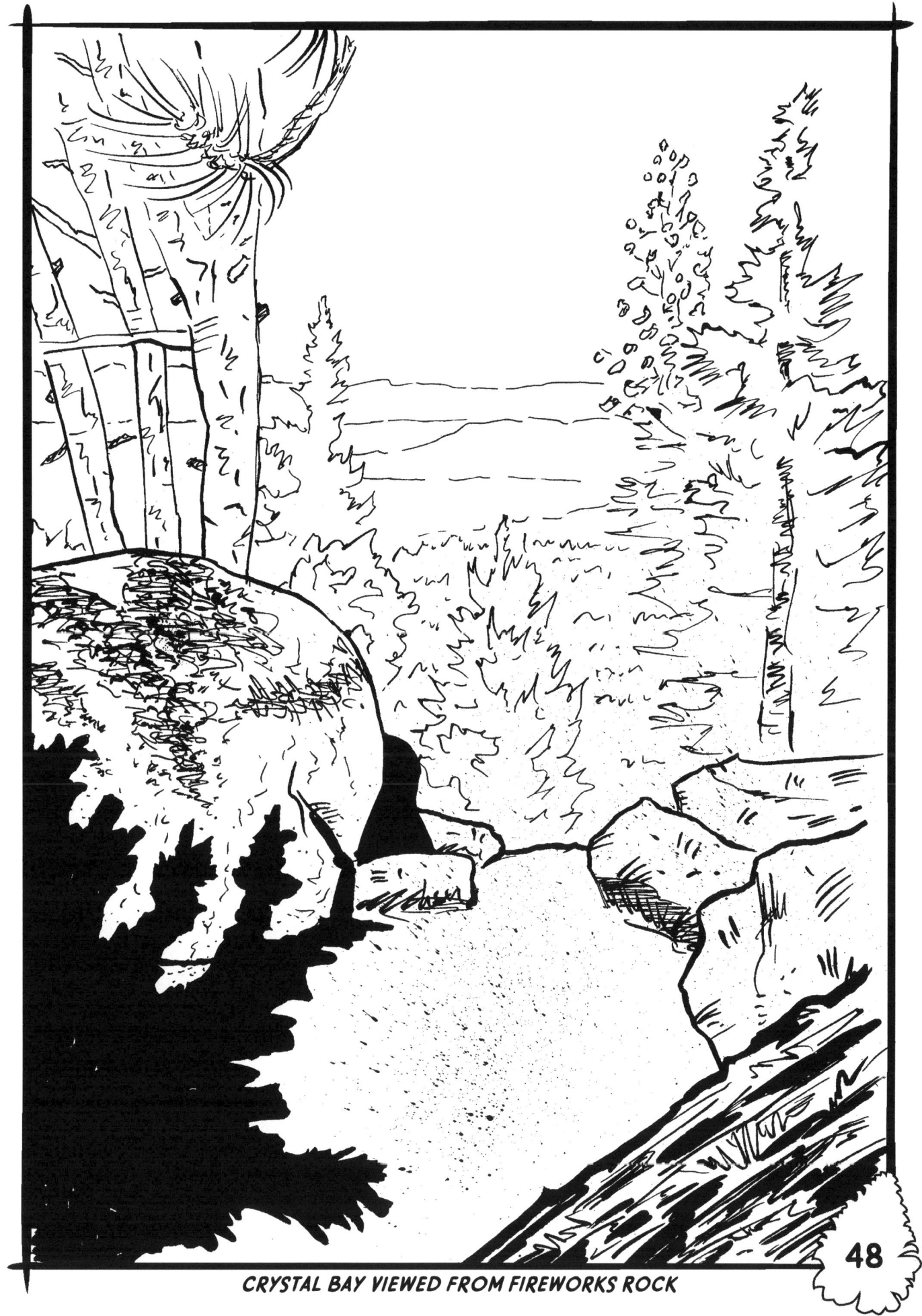

CRYSTAL BAY VIEWED FROM FIREWORKS ROCK

48

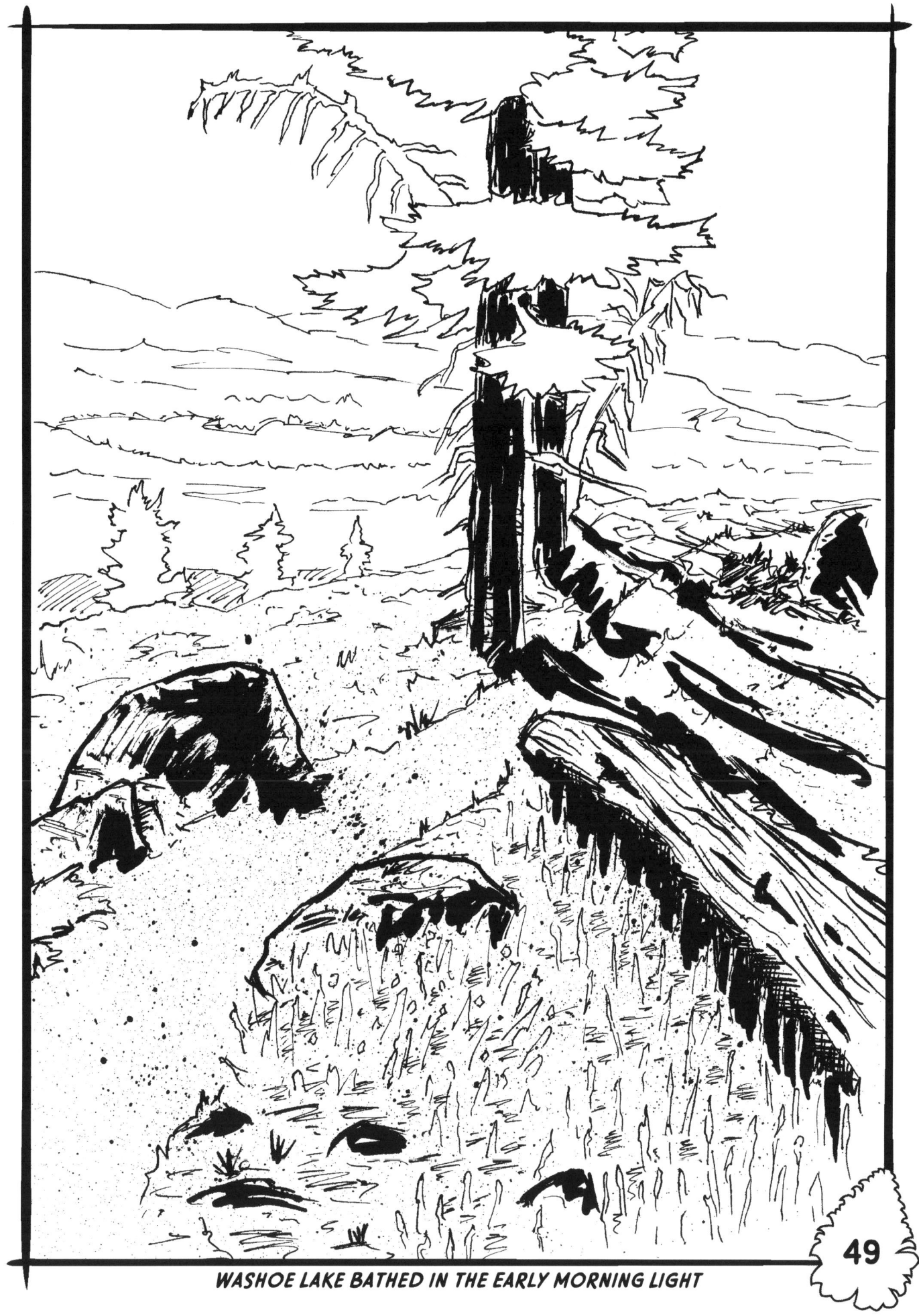

49

WASHOE LAKE BATHED IN THE EARLY MORNING LIGHT

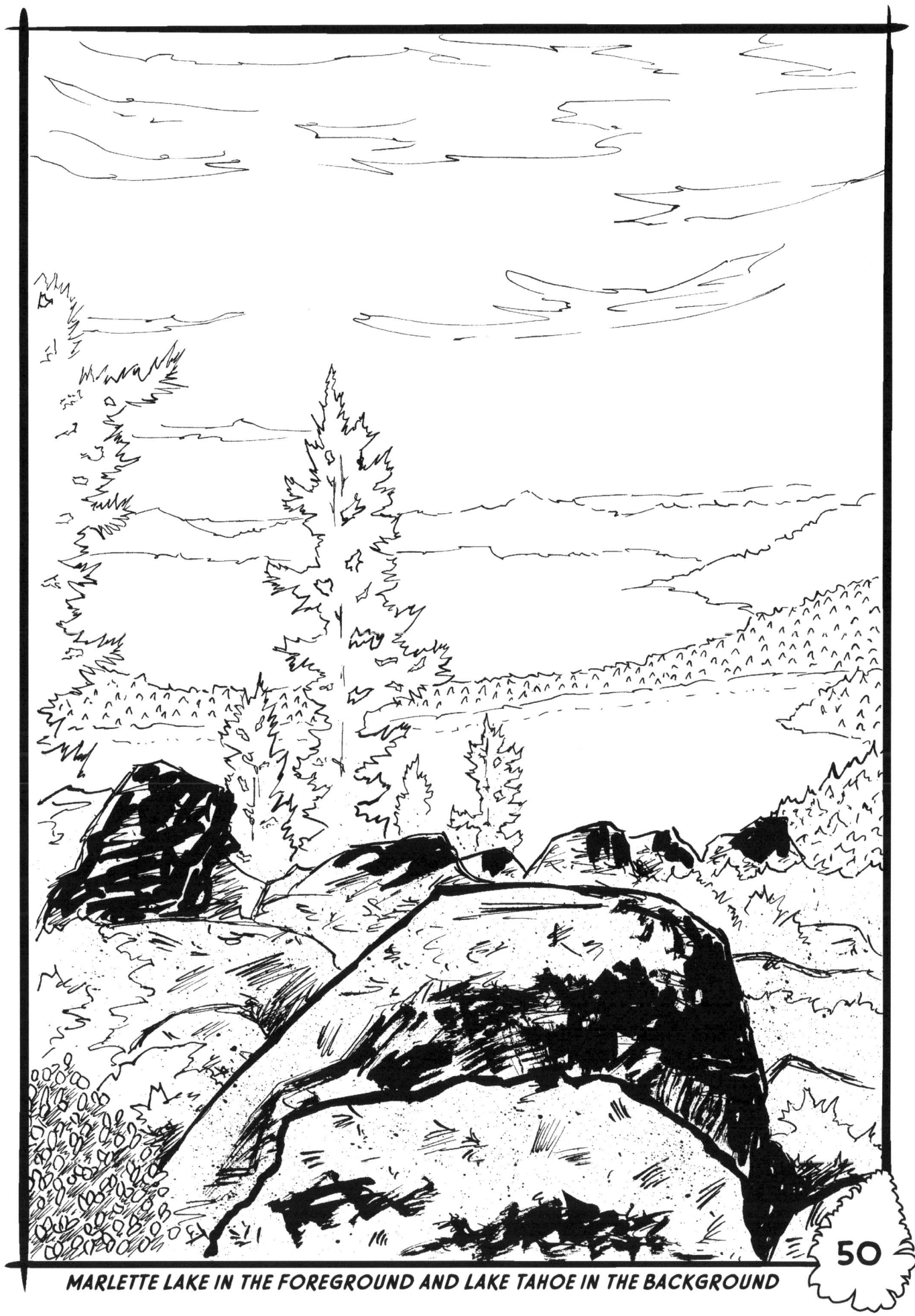

MARLETTE LAKE IN THE FOREGROUND AND LAKE TAHOE IN THE BACKGROUND

50

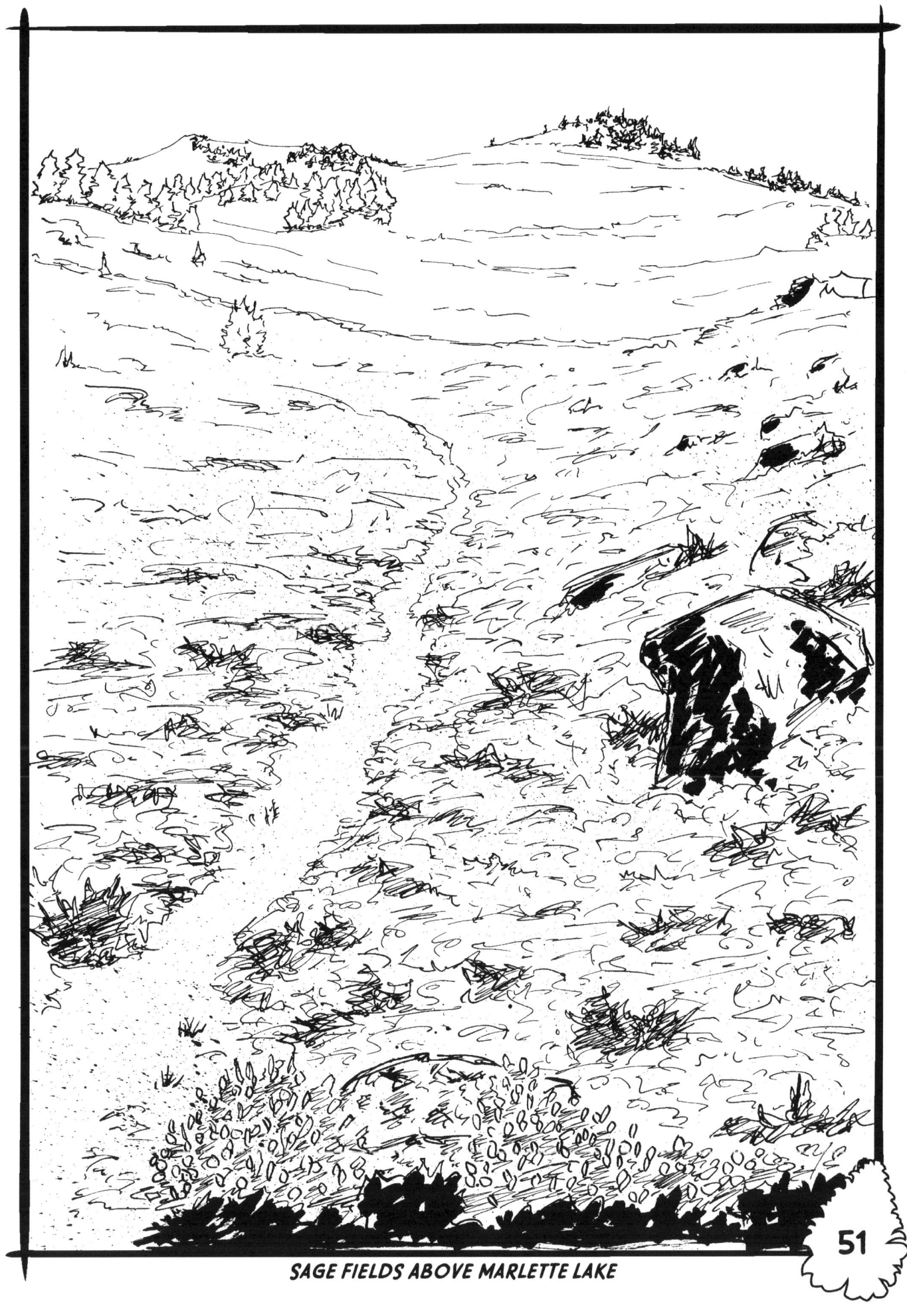

51

SAGE FIELDS ABOVE MARLETTE LAKE

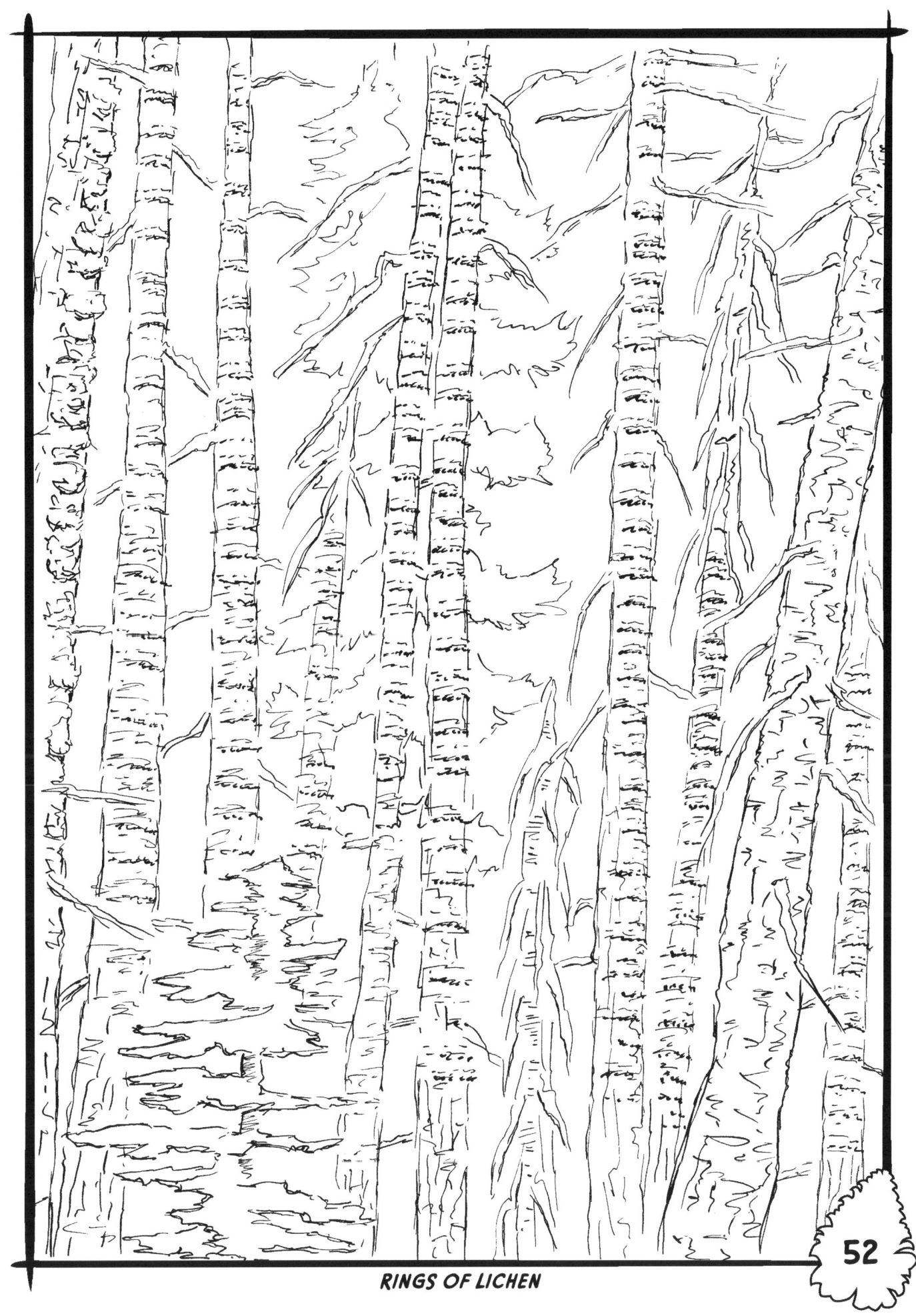

RINGS OF LICHEN

52

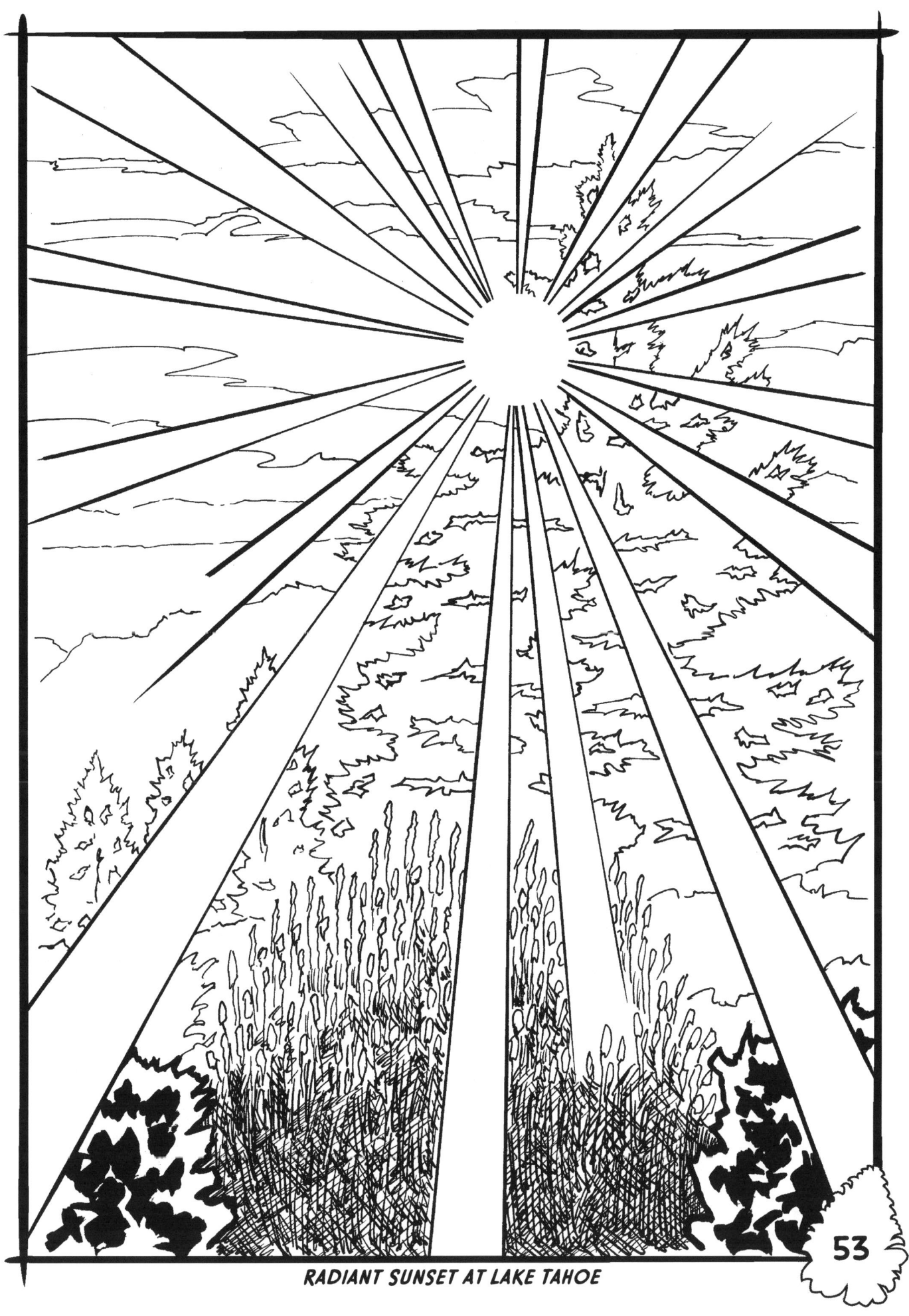

RADIANT SUNSET AT LAKE TAHOE

53

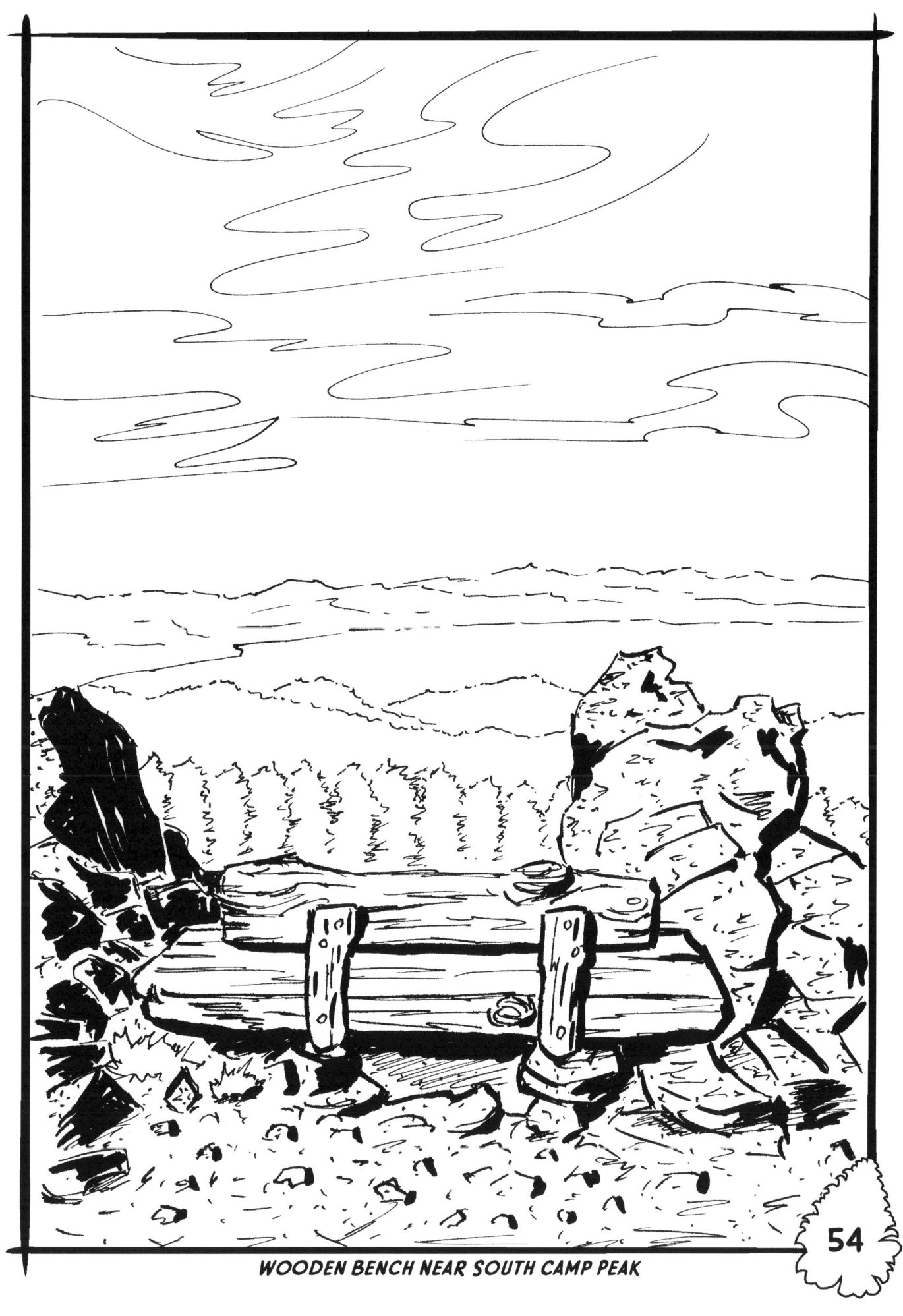

WOODEN BENCH NEAR SOUTH CAMP PEAK

54

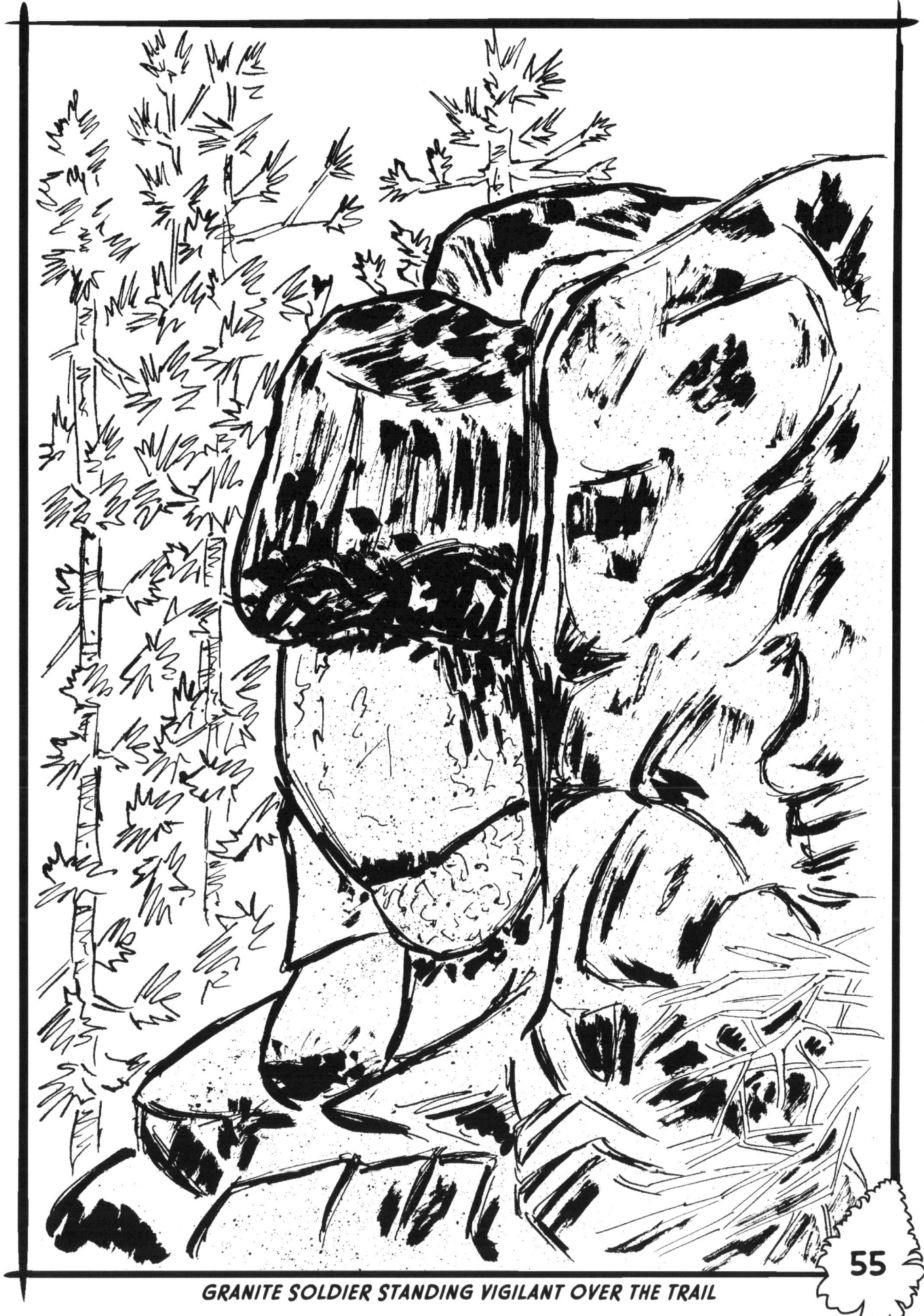

GRANITE SOLDIER STANDING VIGILANT OVER THE TRAIL

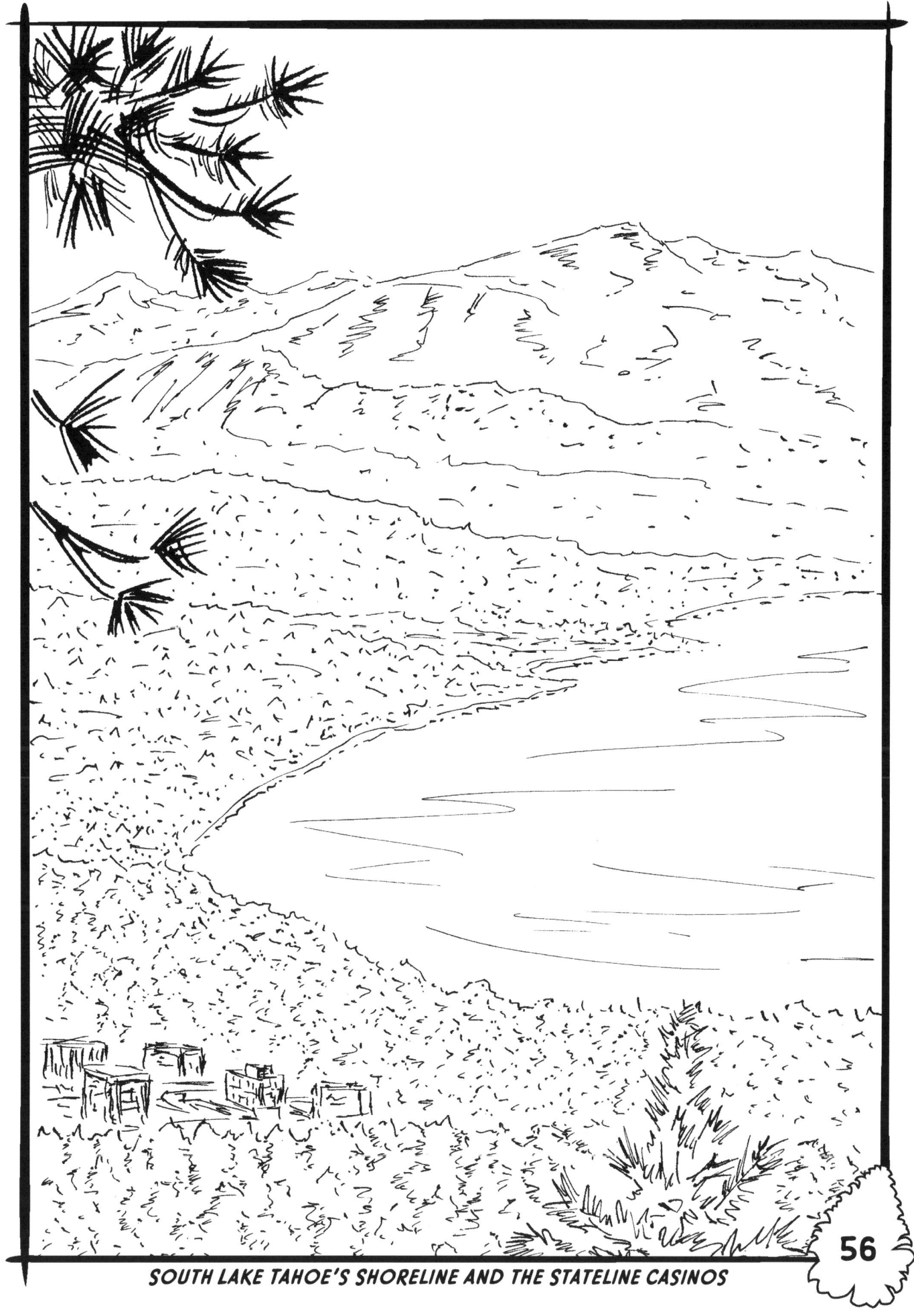

SOUTH LAKE TAHOE'S SHORELINE AND THE STATELINE CASINOS

56

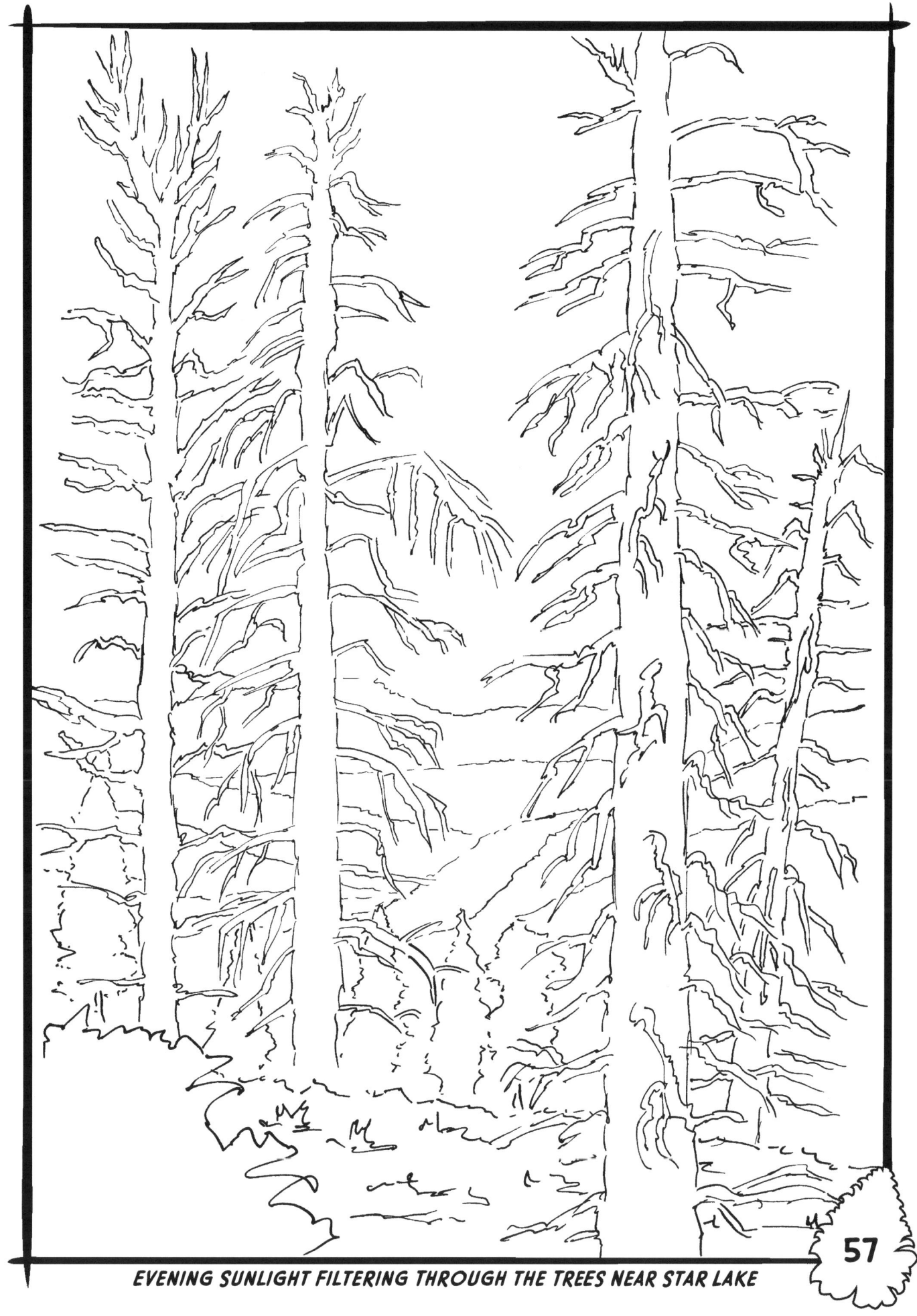

57

EVENING SUNLIGHT FILTERING THROUGH THE TREES NEAR STAR LAKE

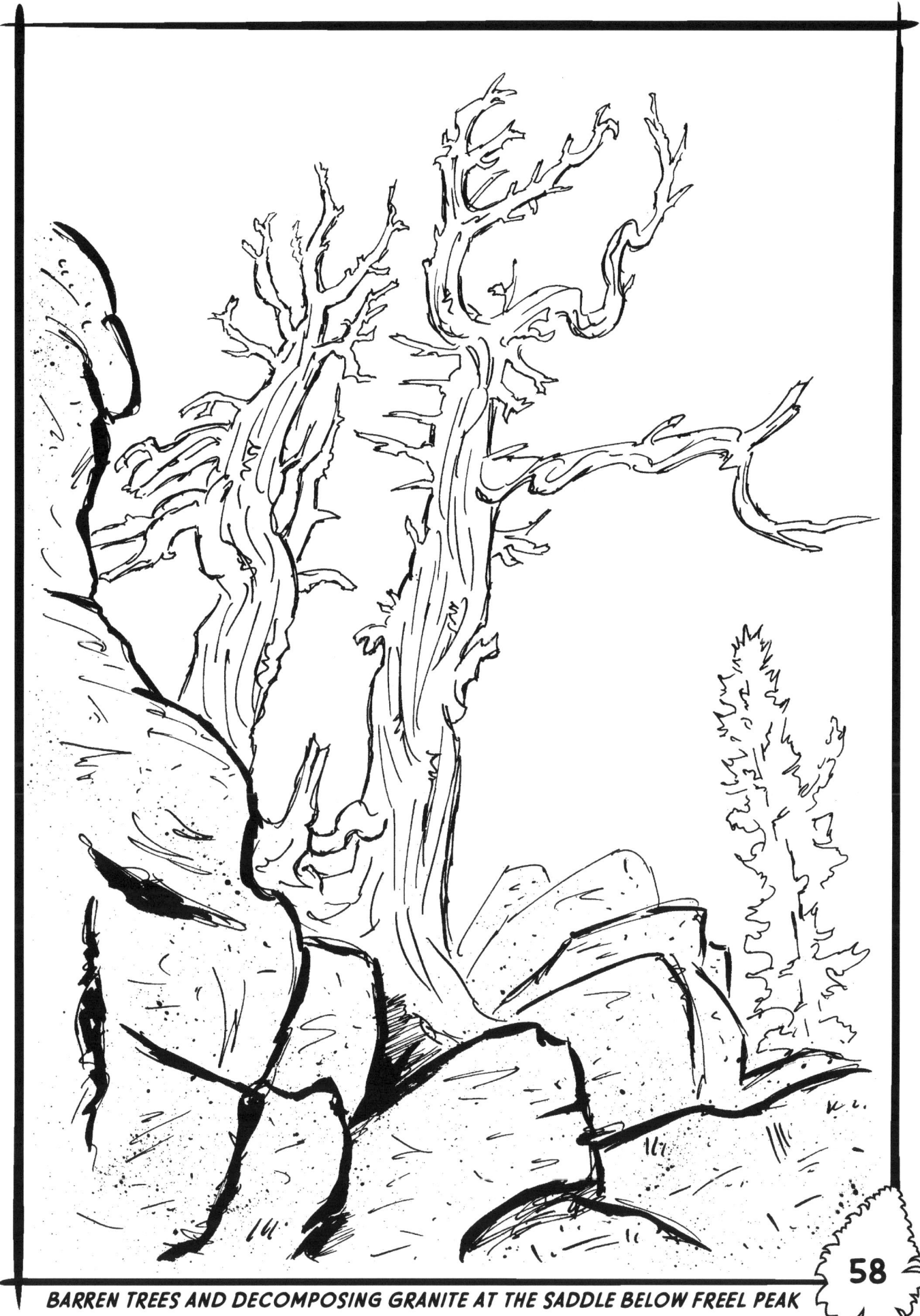

58

BARREN TREES AND DECOMPOSING GRANITE AT THE SADDLE BELOW FREEL PEAK

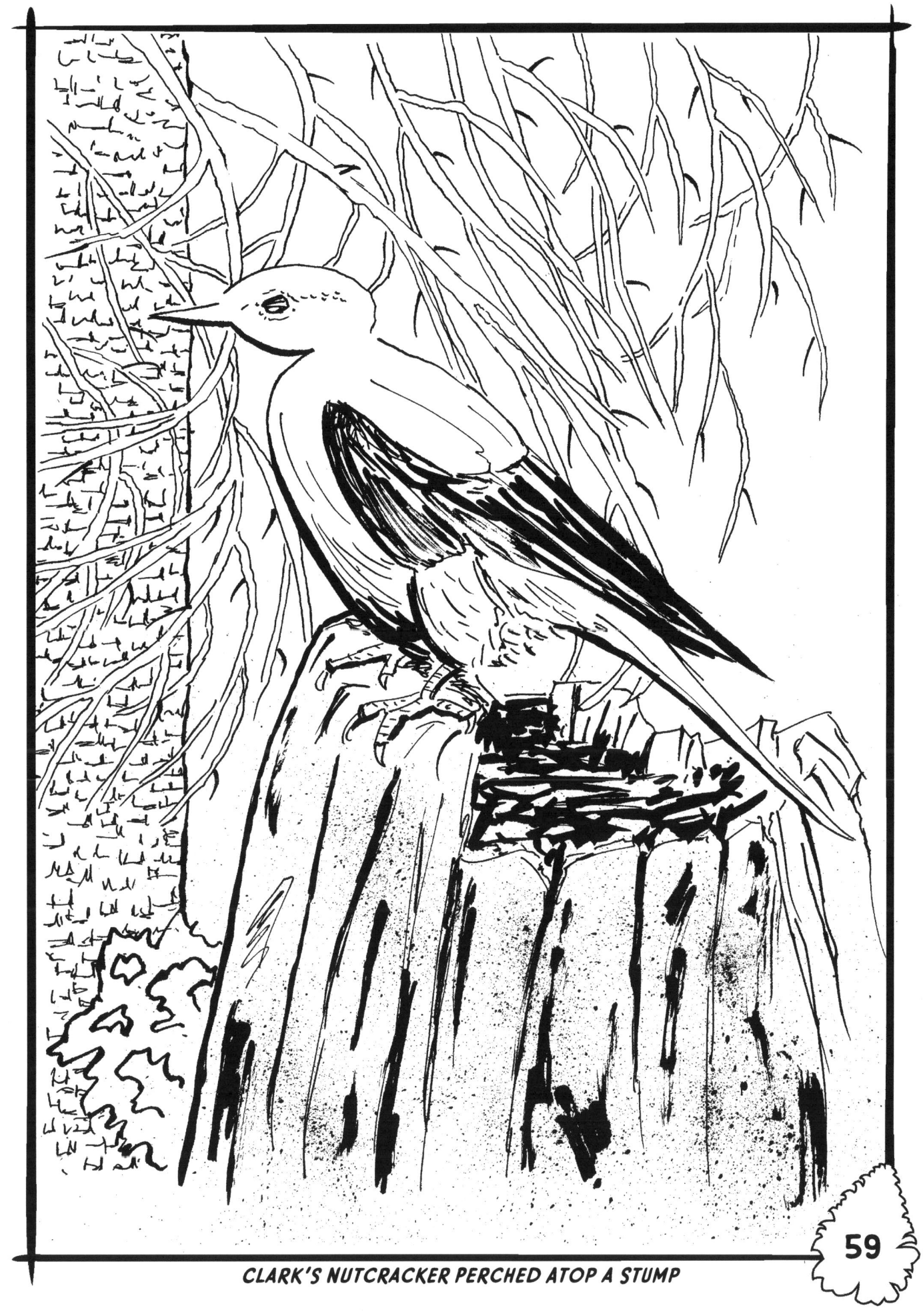

CLARK'S NUTCRACKER PERCHED ATOP A STUMP

59

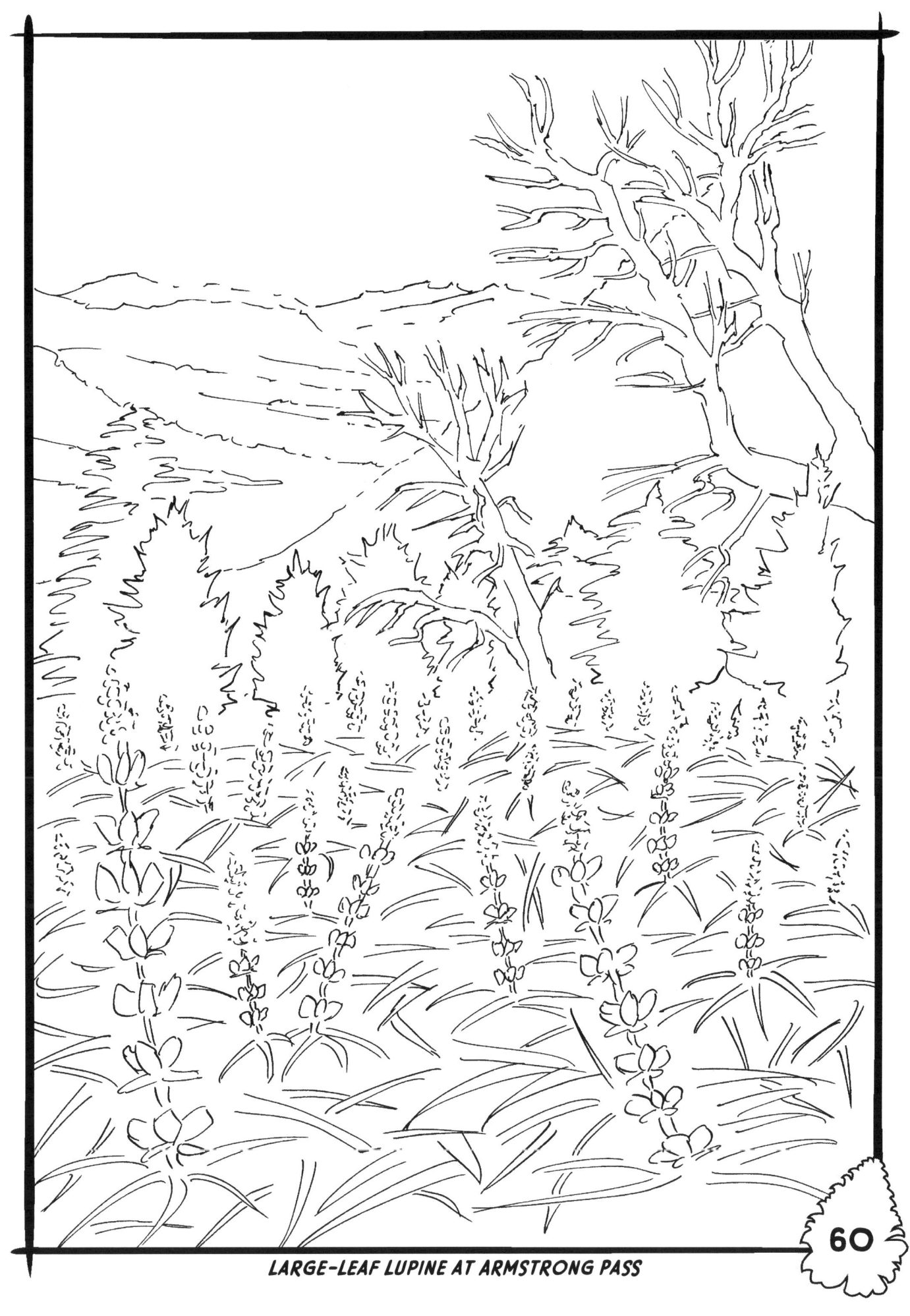

LARGE-LEAF LUPINE AT ARMSTRONG PASS

60

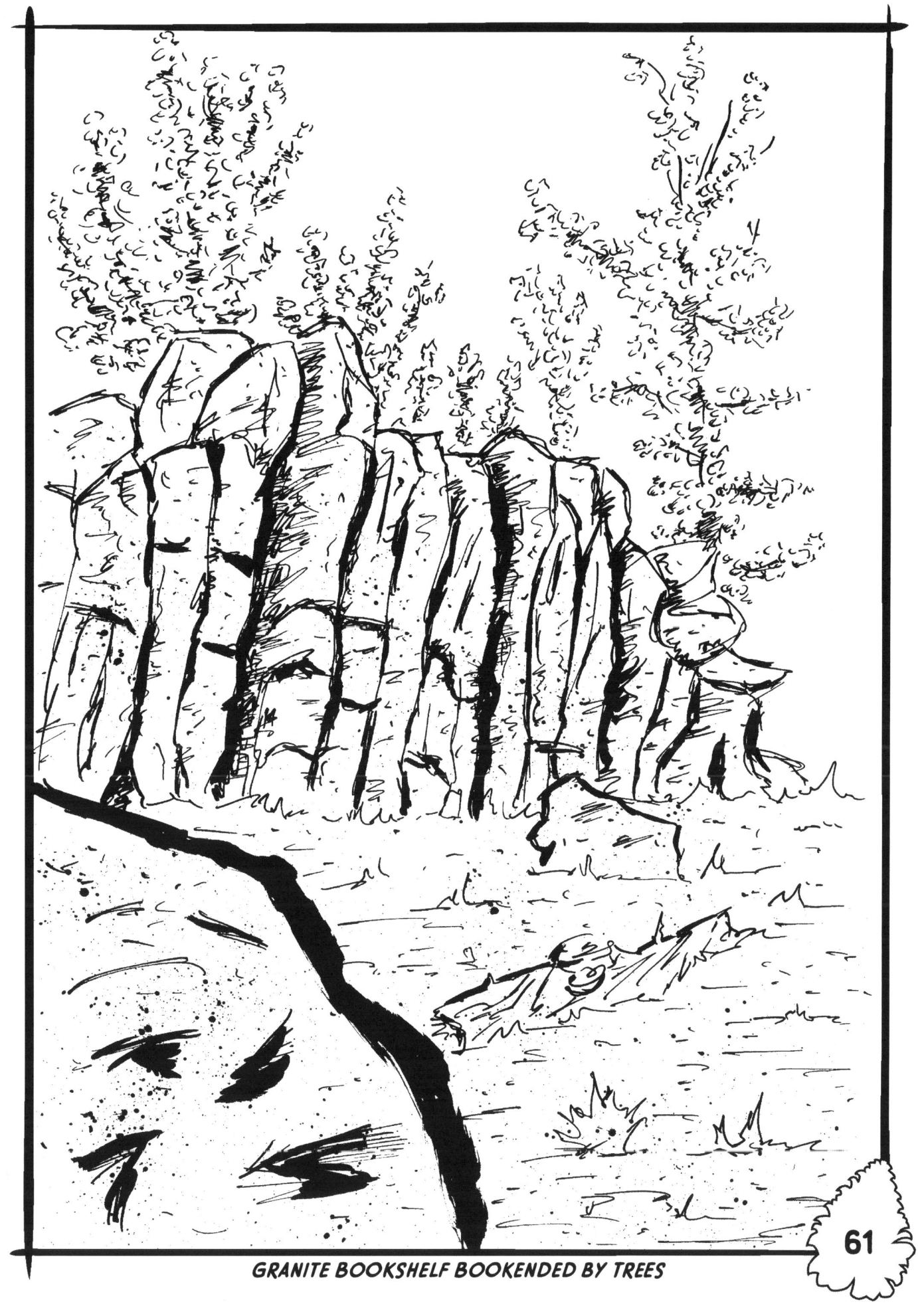

GRANITE BOOKSHELF BOOKENDED BY TREES

61

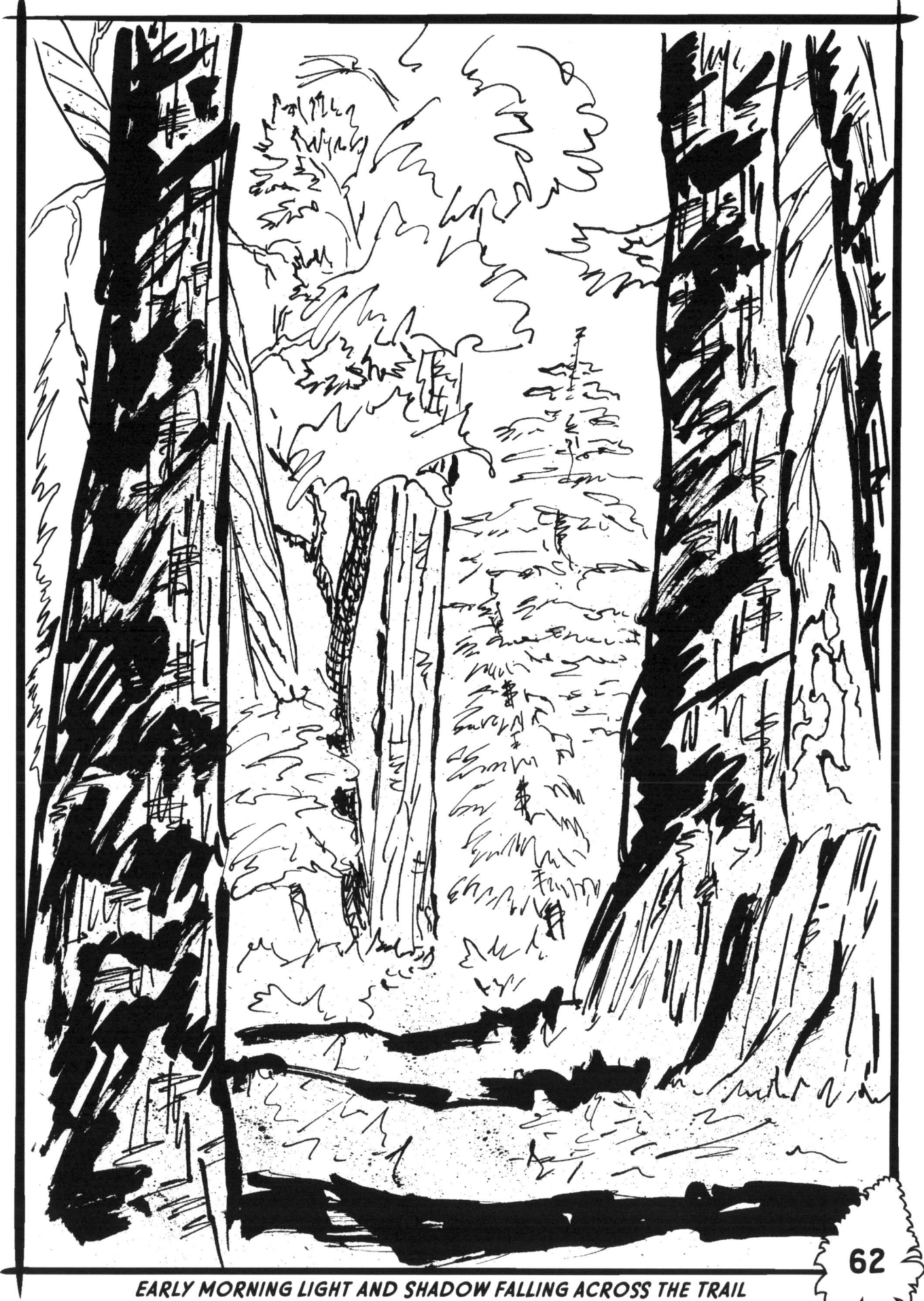

EARLY MORNING LIGHT AND SHADOW FALLING ACROSS THE TRAIL

62

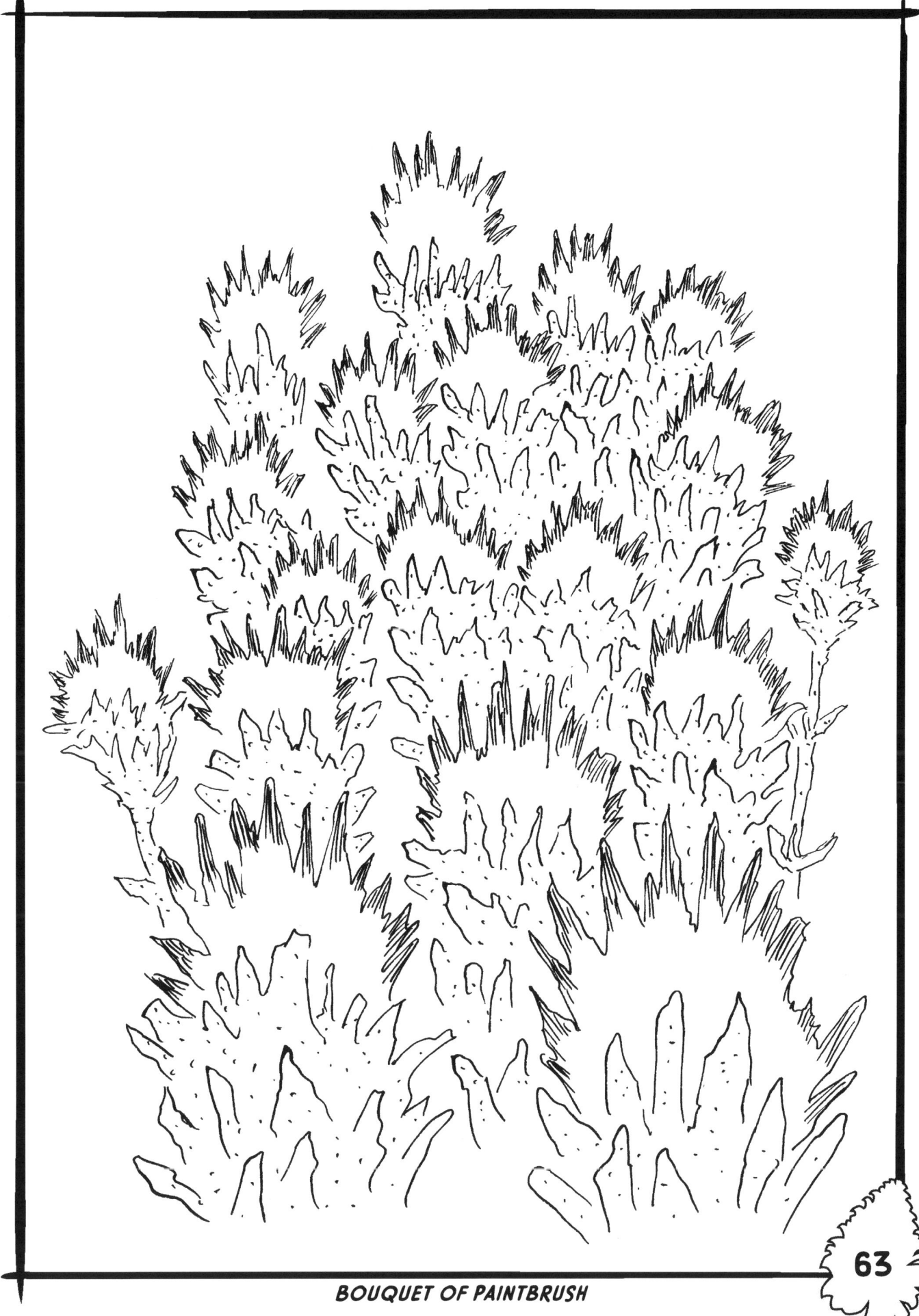

BOUQUET OF PAINTBRUSH

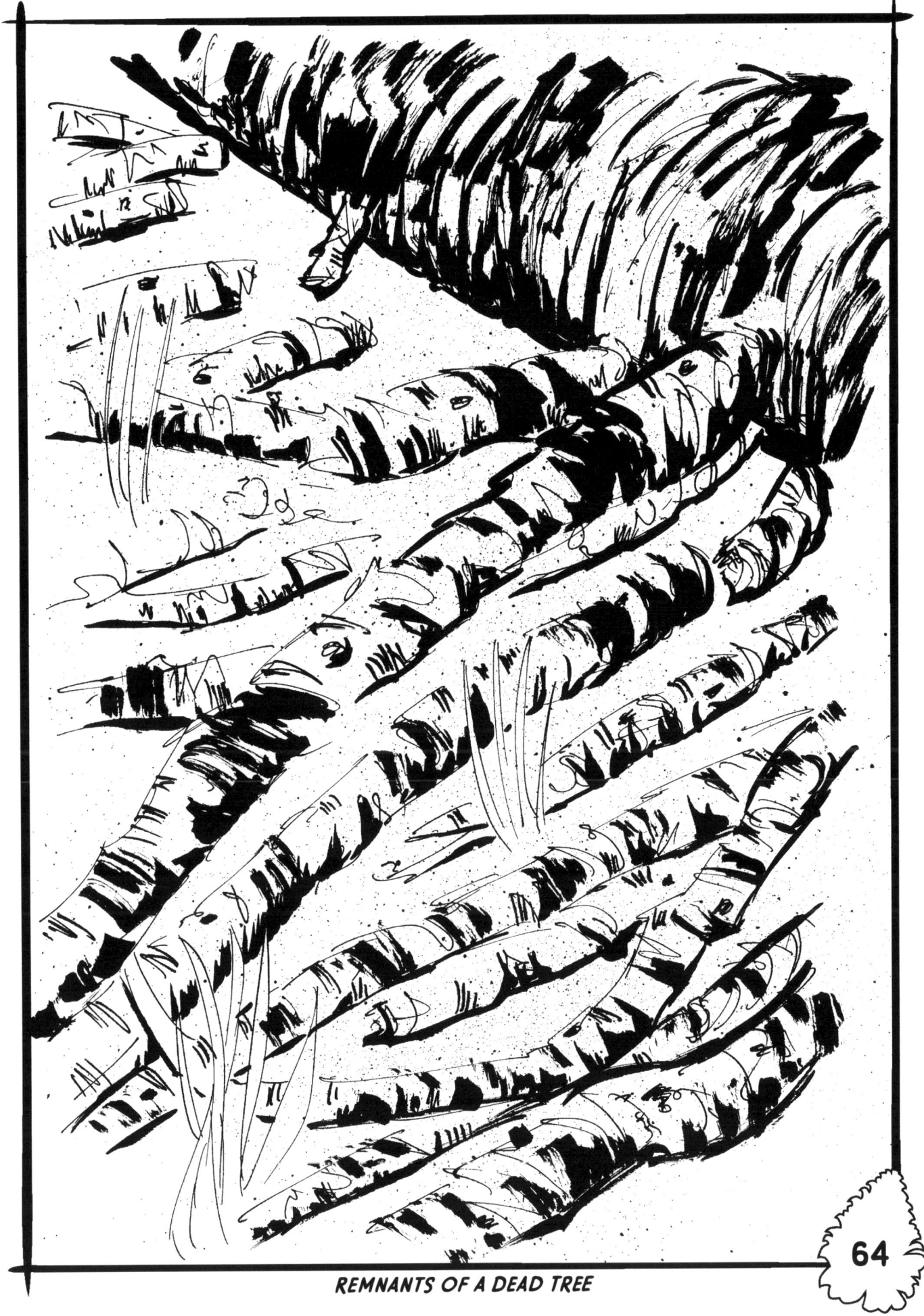

REMNANTS OF A DEAD TREE

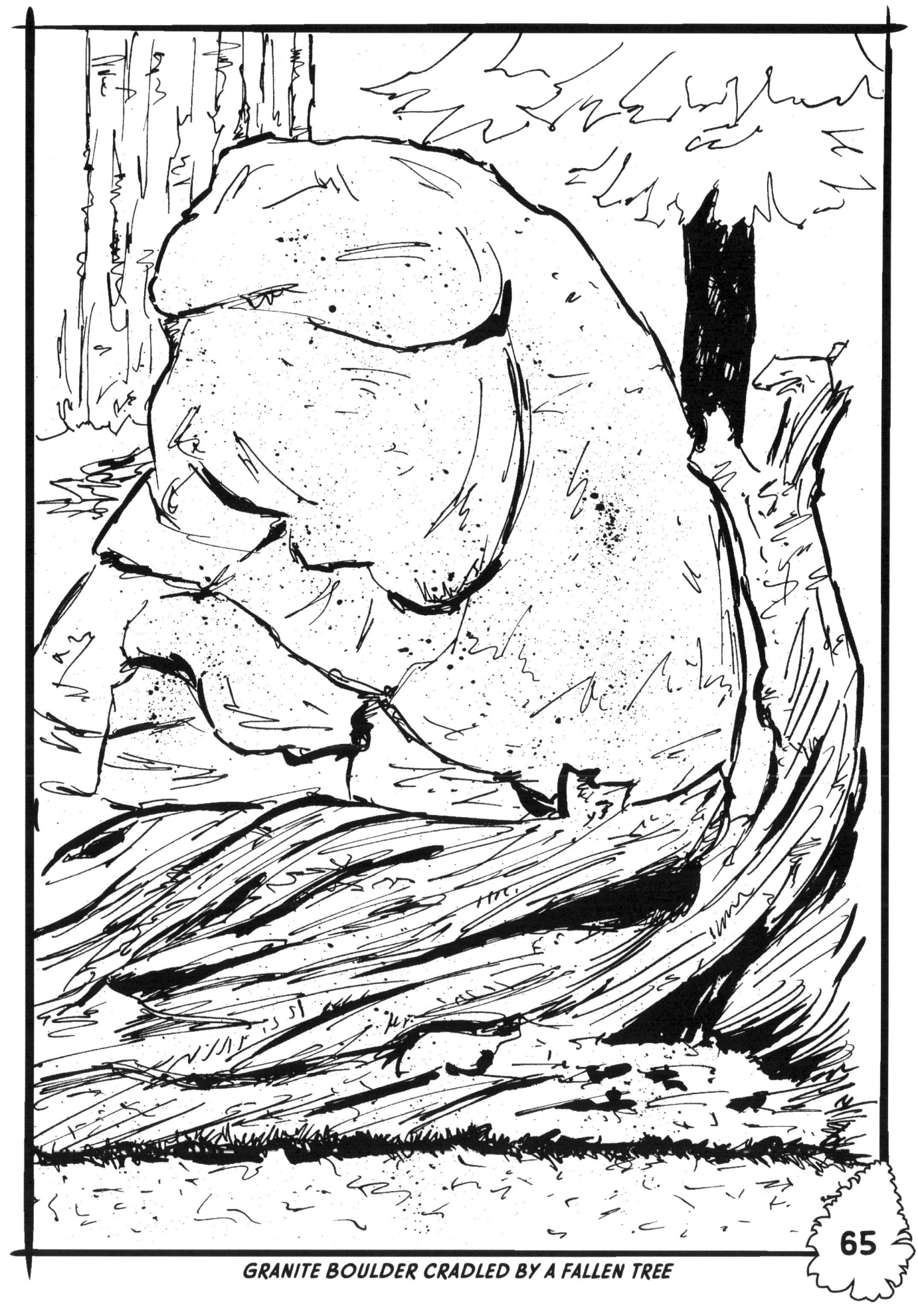

GRANITE BOULDER CRADLED BY A FALLEN TREE

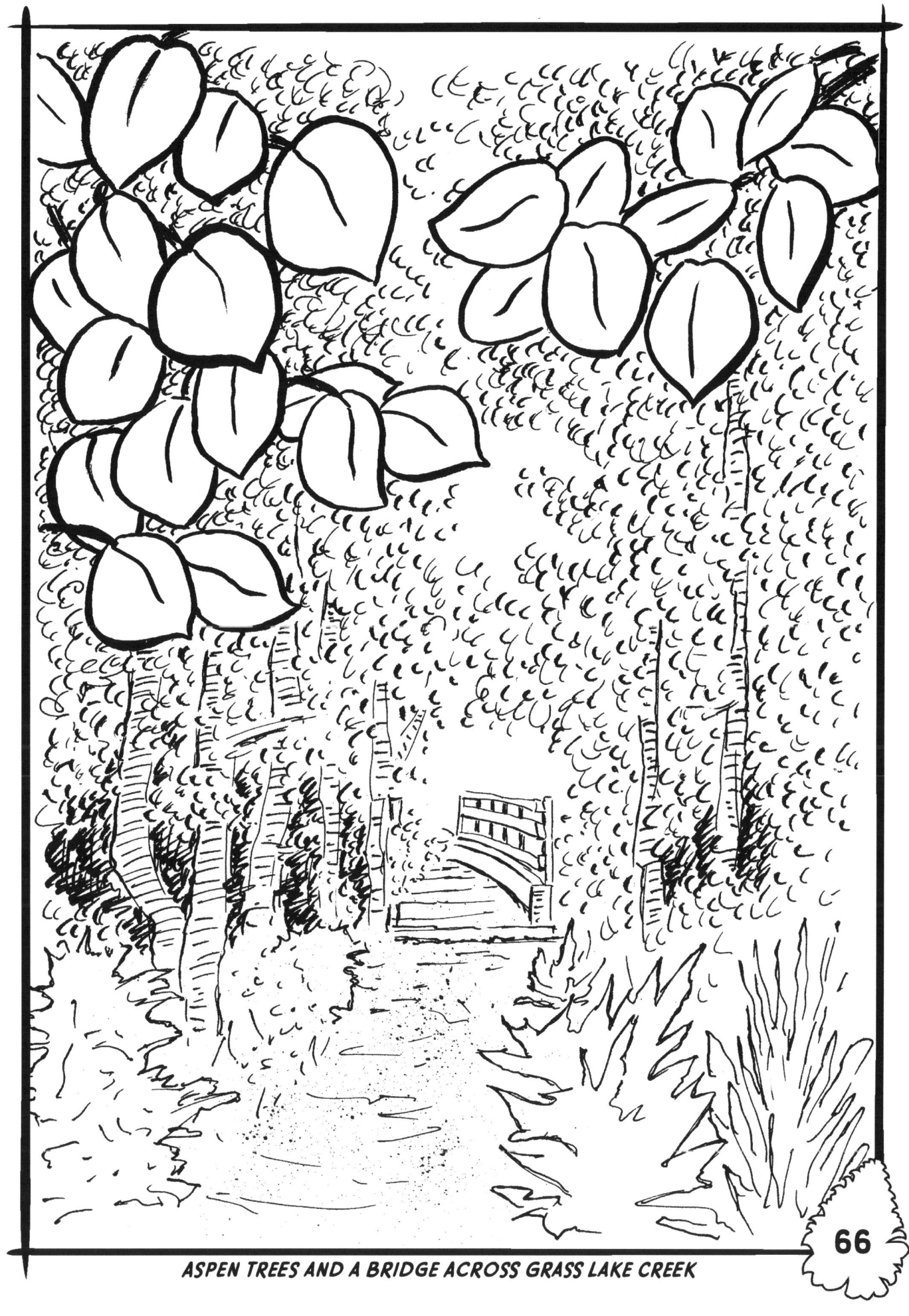

ASPEN TREES AND A BRIDGE ACROSS GRASS LAKE CREEK

66

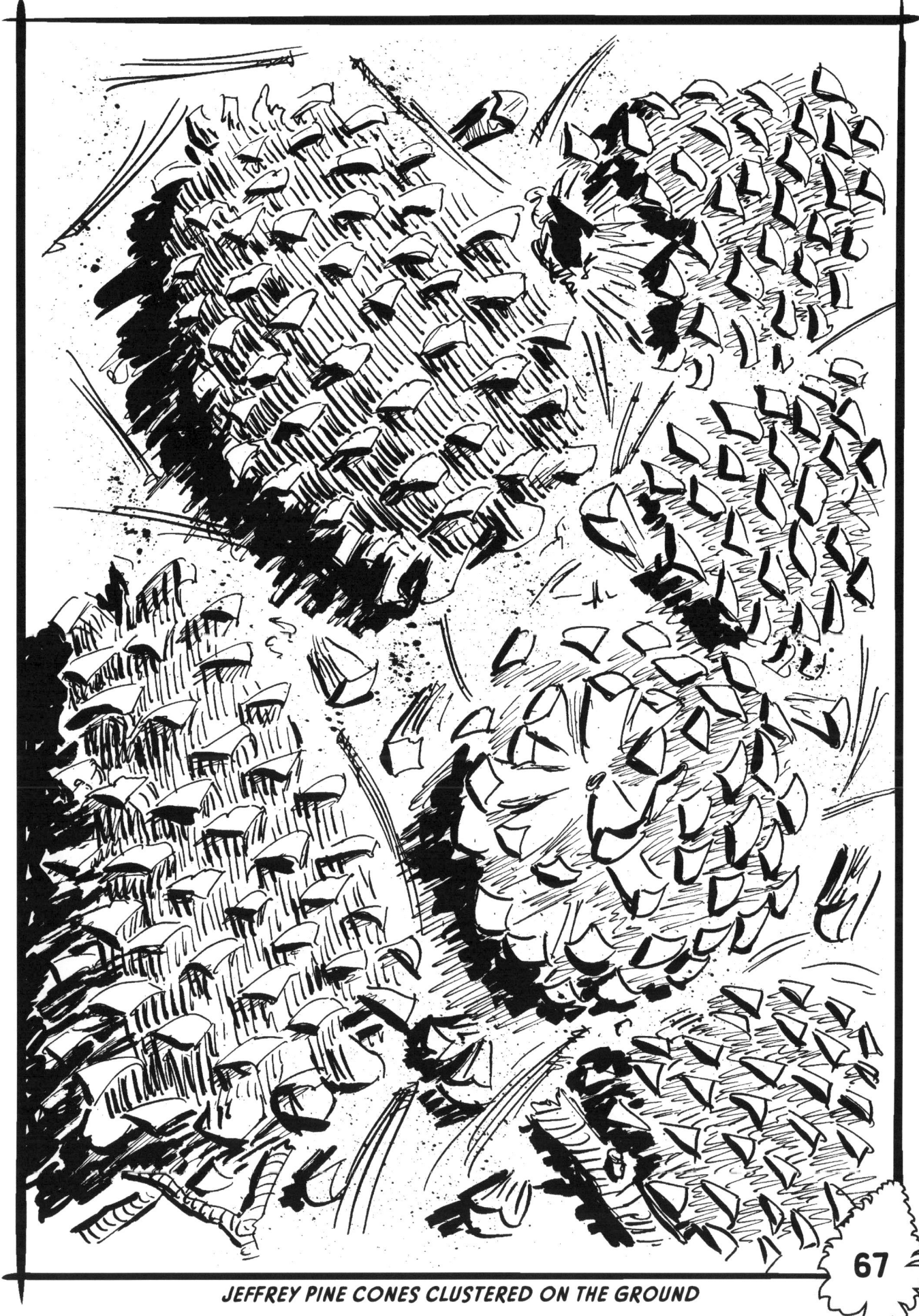

JEFFREY PINE CONES CLUSTERED ON THE GROUND

67

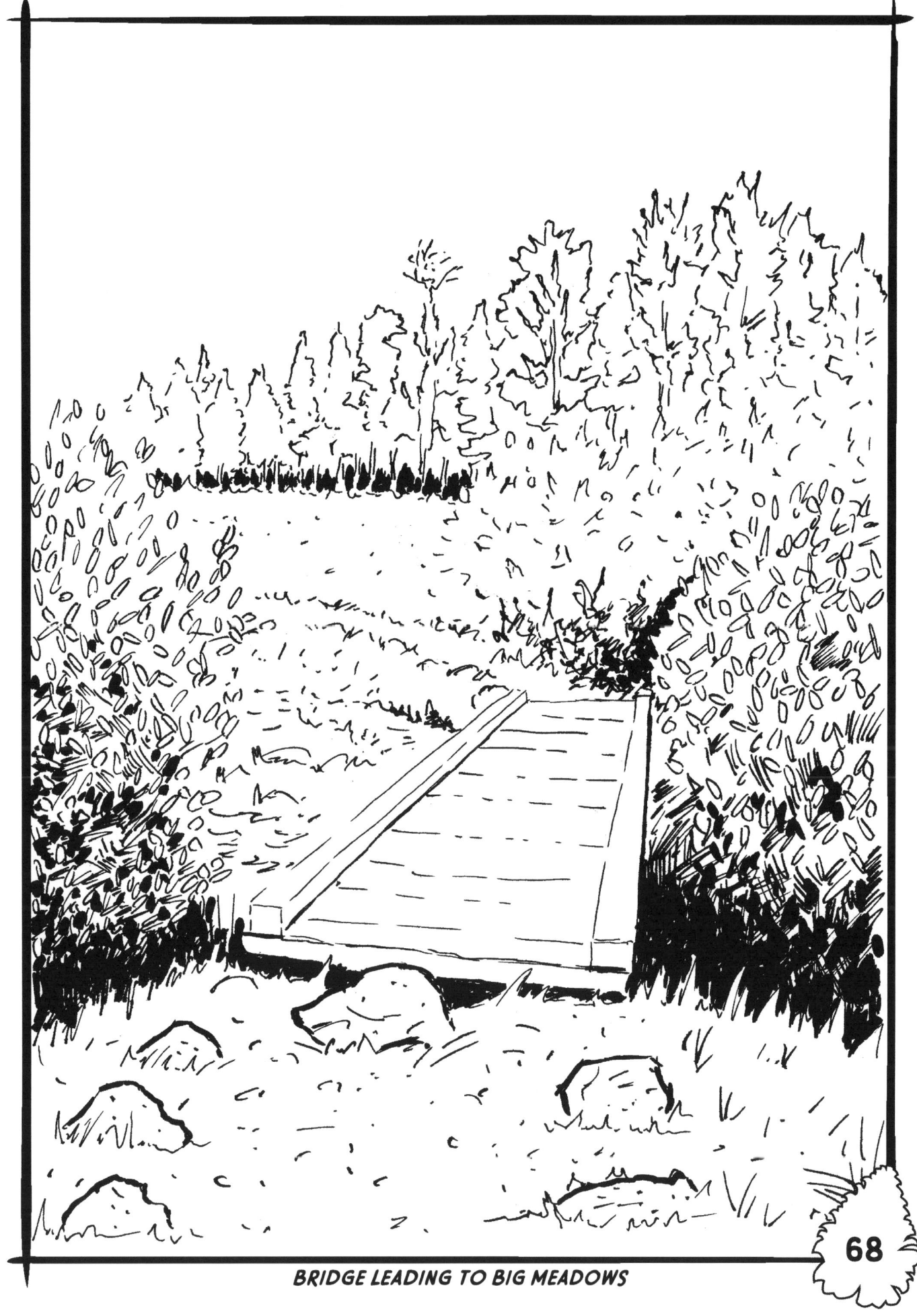

68

BRIDGE LEADING TO BIG MEADOWS

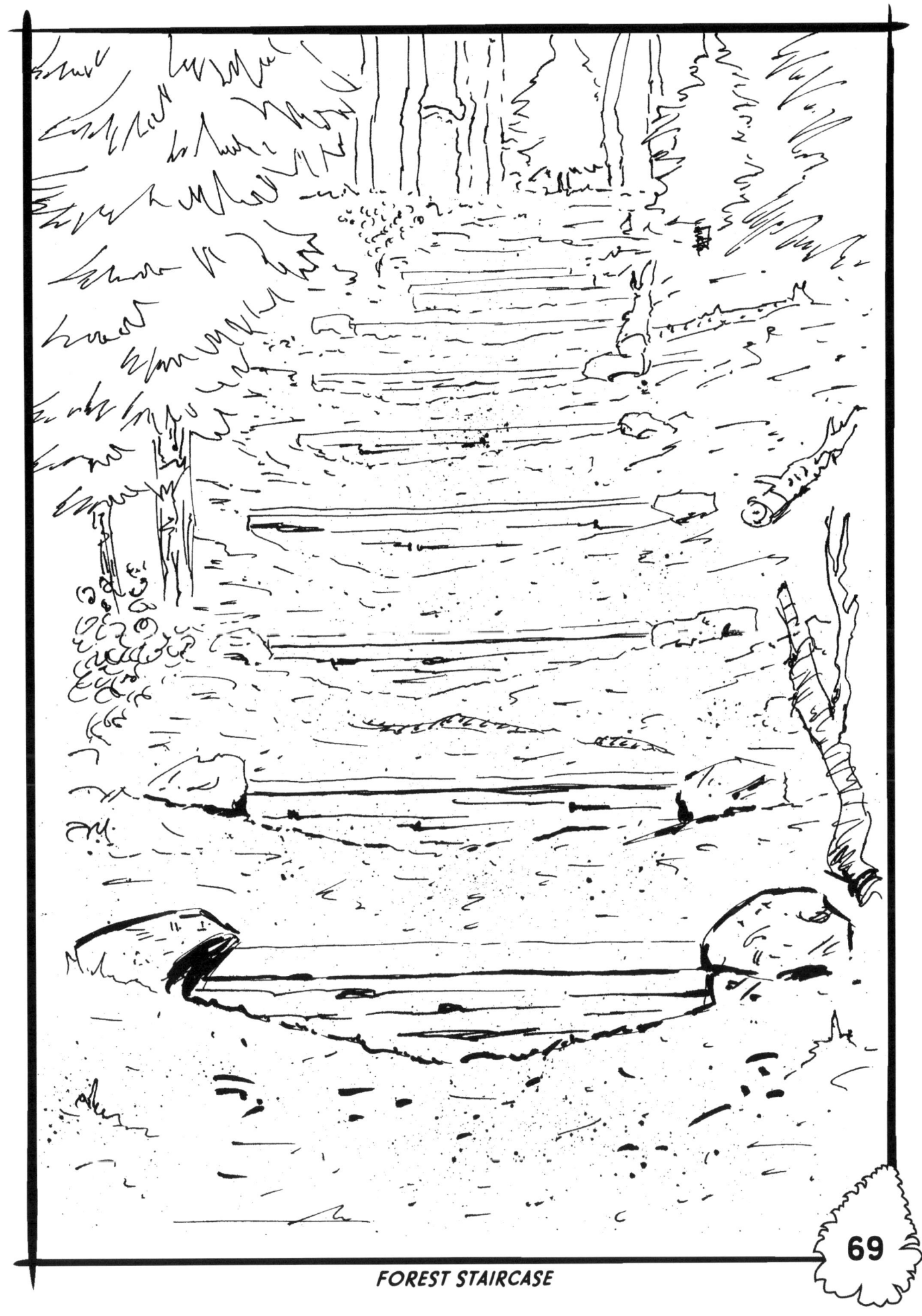

69

FOREST STAIRCASE

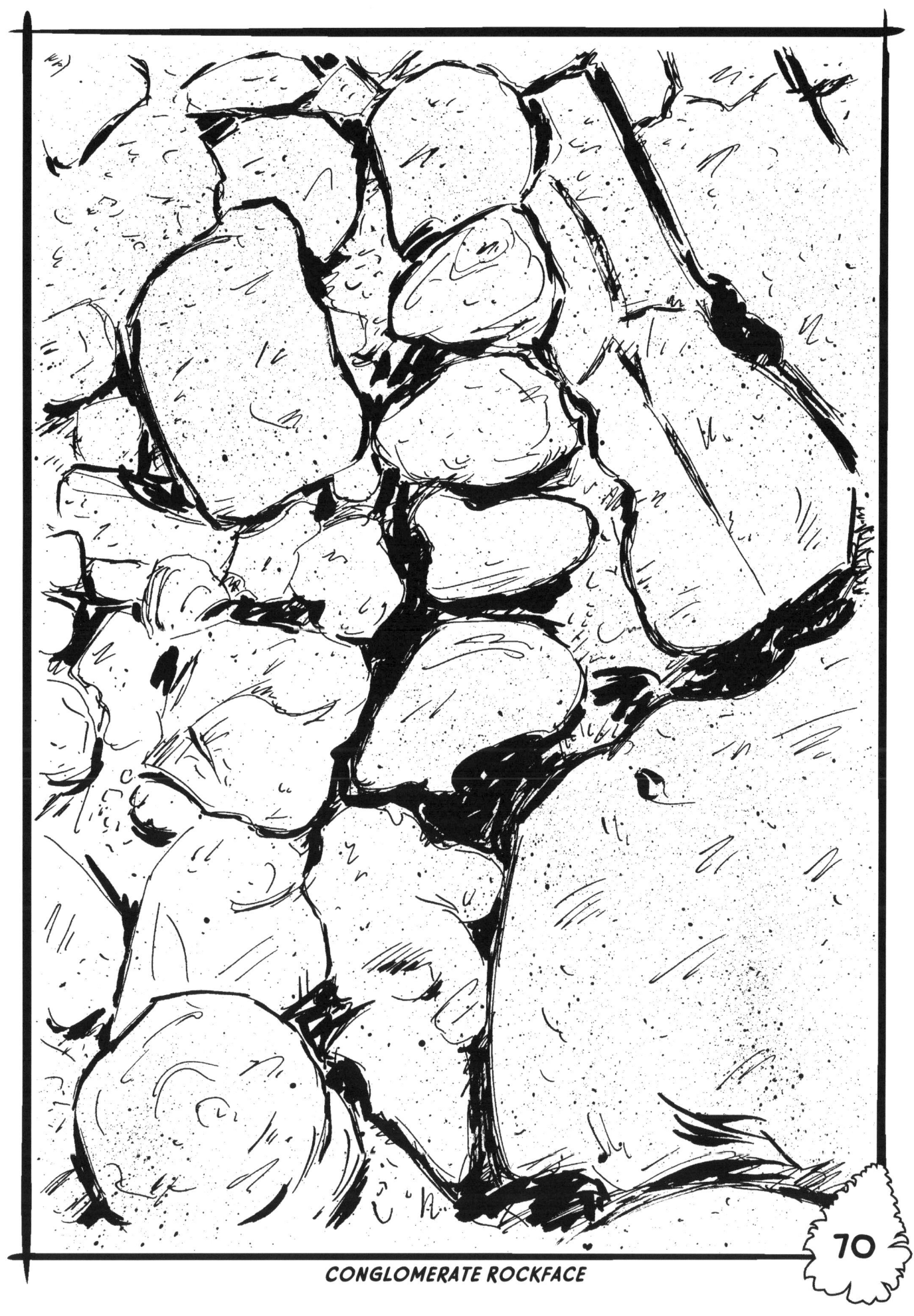

CONGLOMERATE ROCKFACE

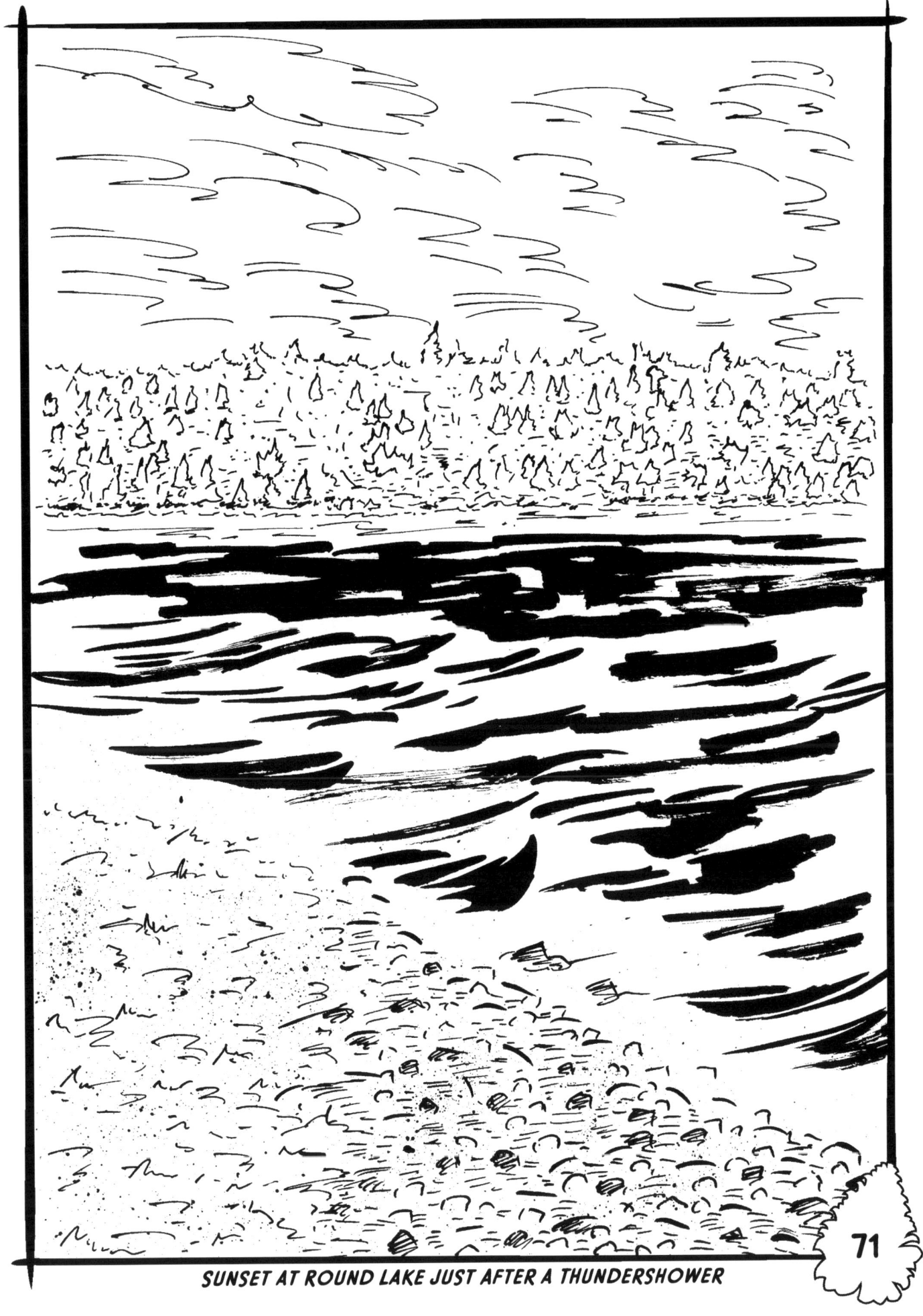

SUNSET AT ROUND LAKE JUST AFTER A THUNDERSHOWER

71

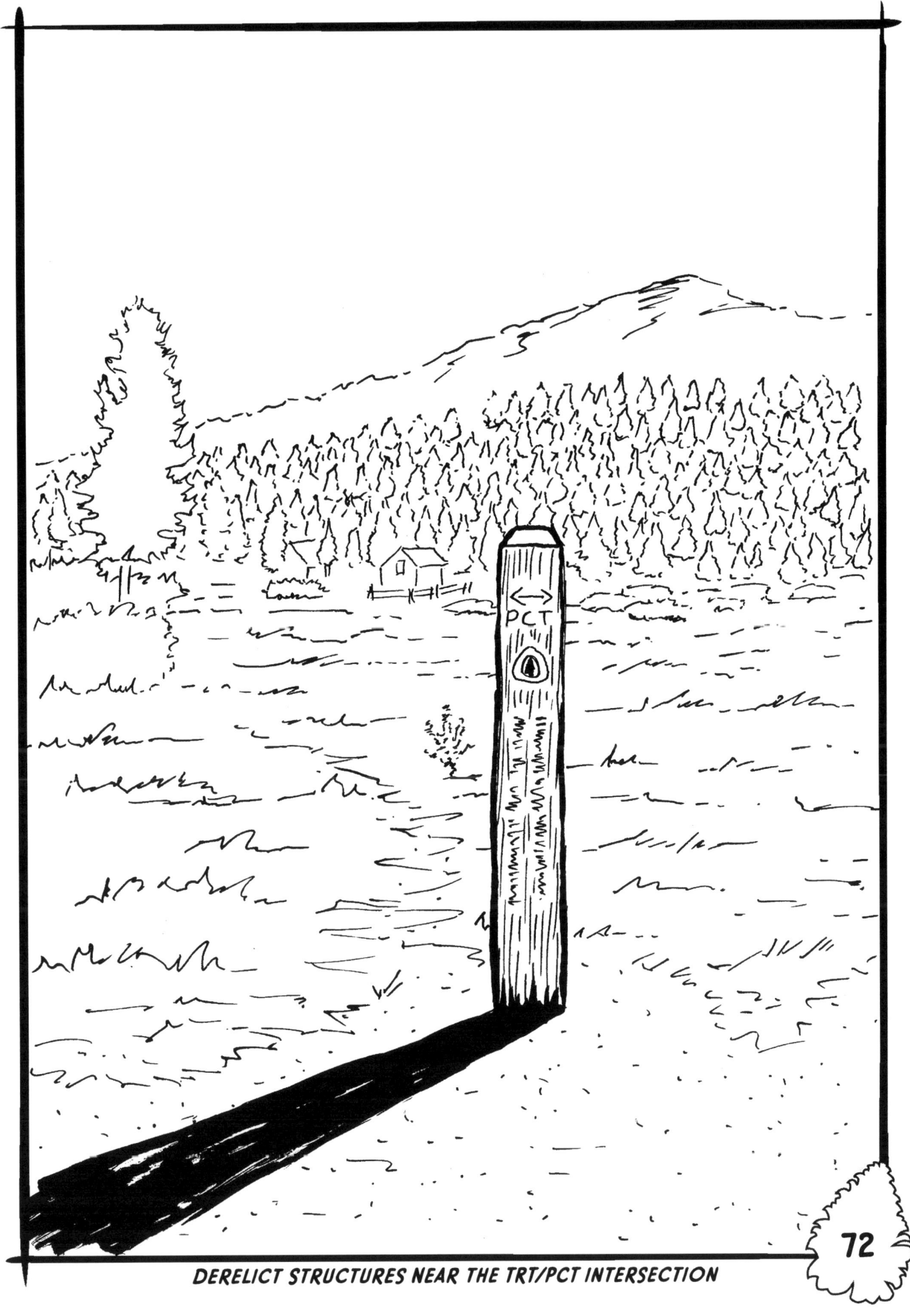

DERELICT STRUCTURES NEAR THE TRT/PCT INTERSECTION

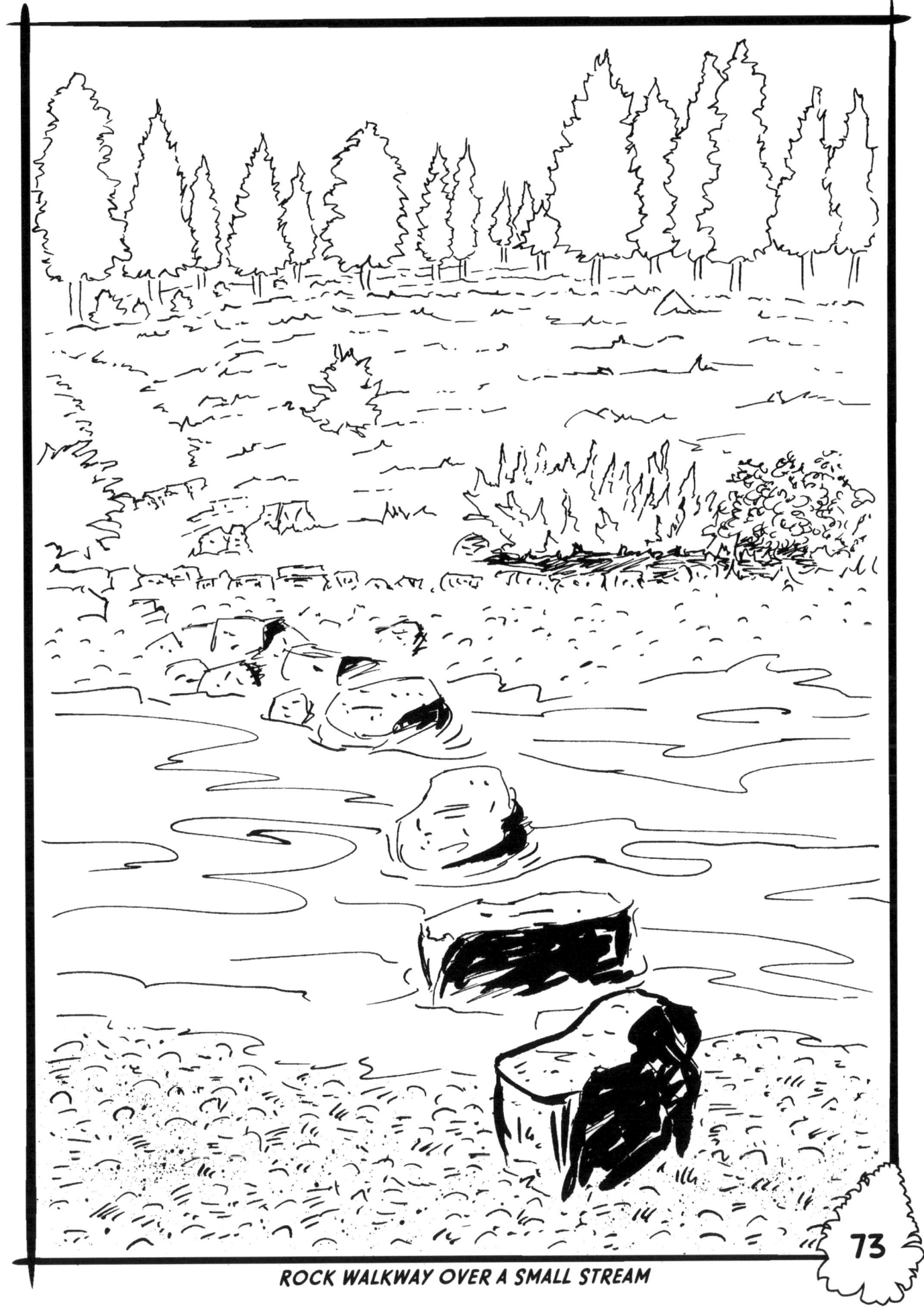

73

ROCK WALKWAY OVER A SMALL STREAM

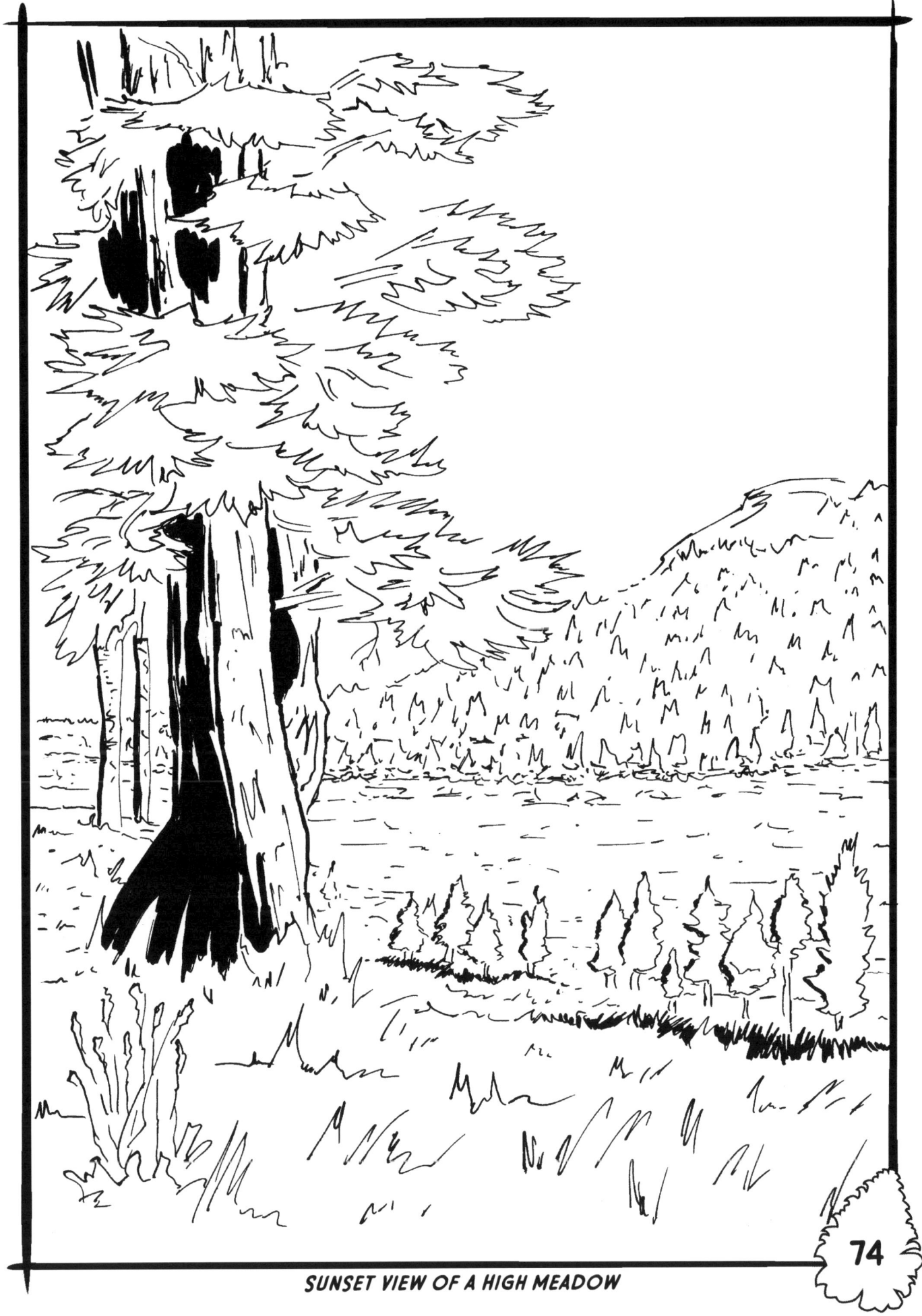

SUNSET VIEW OF A HIGH MEADOW

74

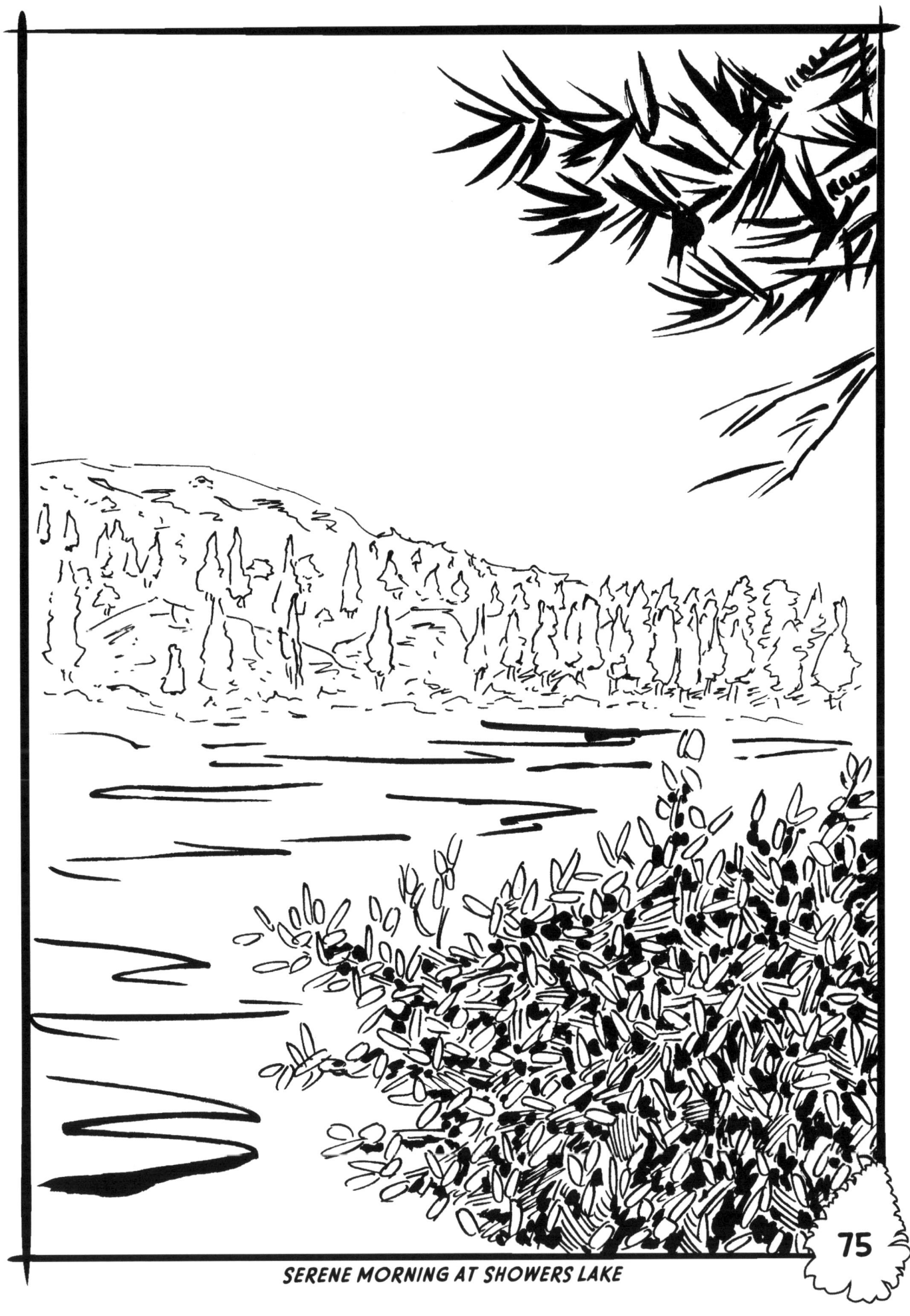

75

SERENE MORNING AT SHOWERS LAKE

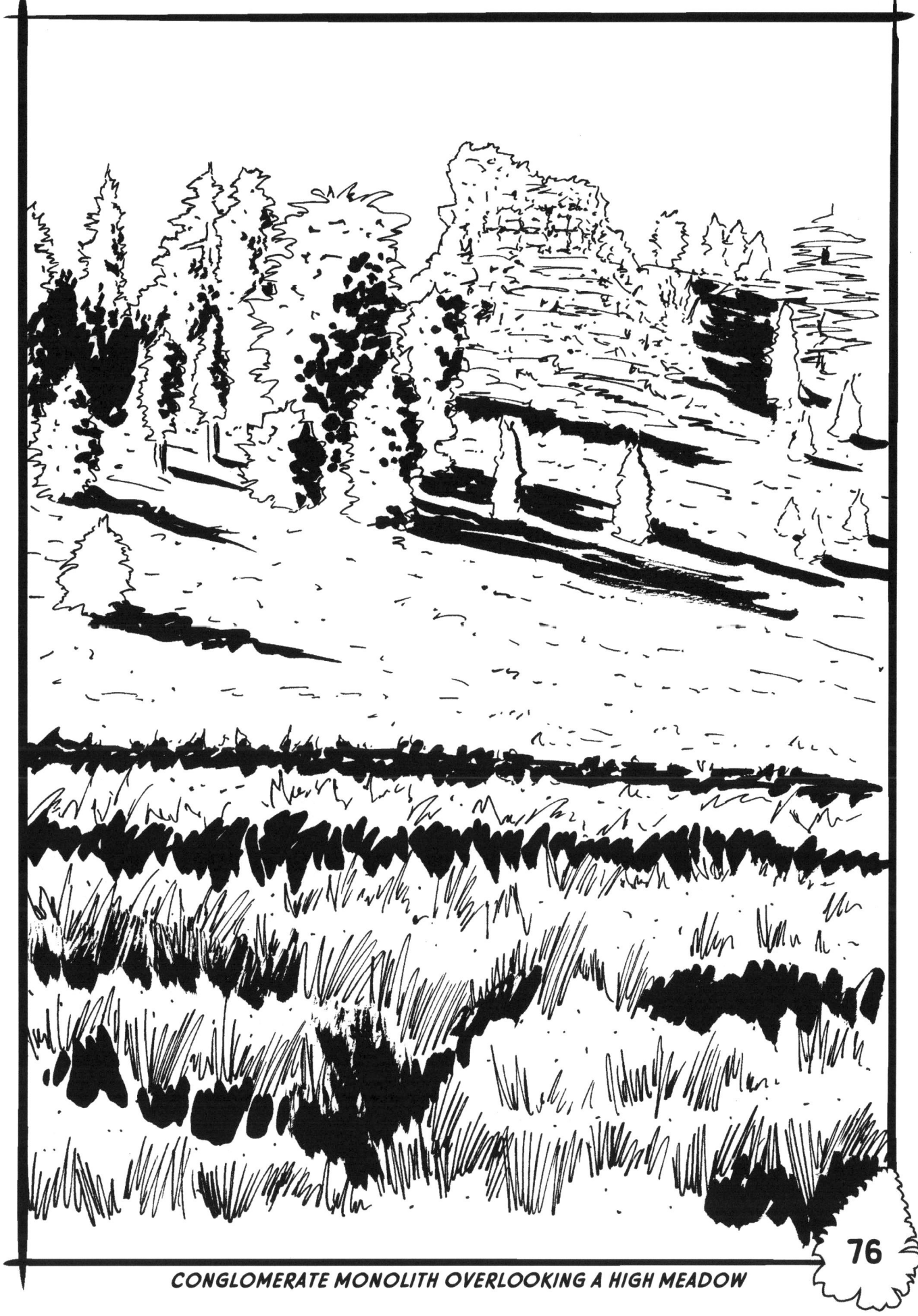

76

CONGLOMERATE MONOLITH OVERLOOKING A HIGH MEADOW

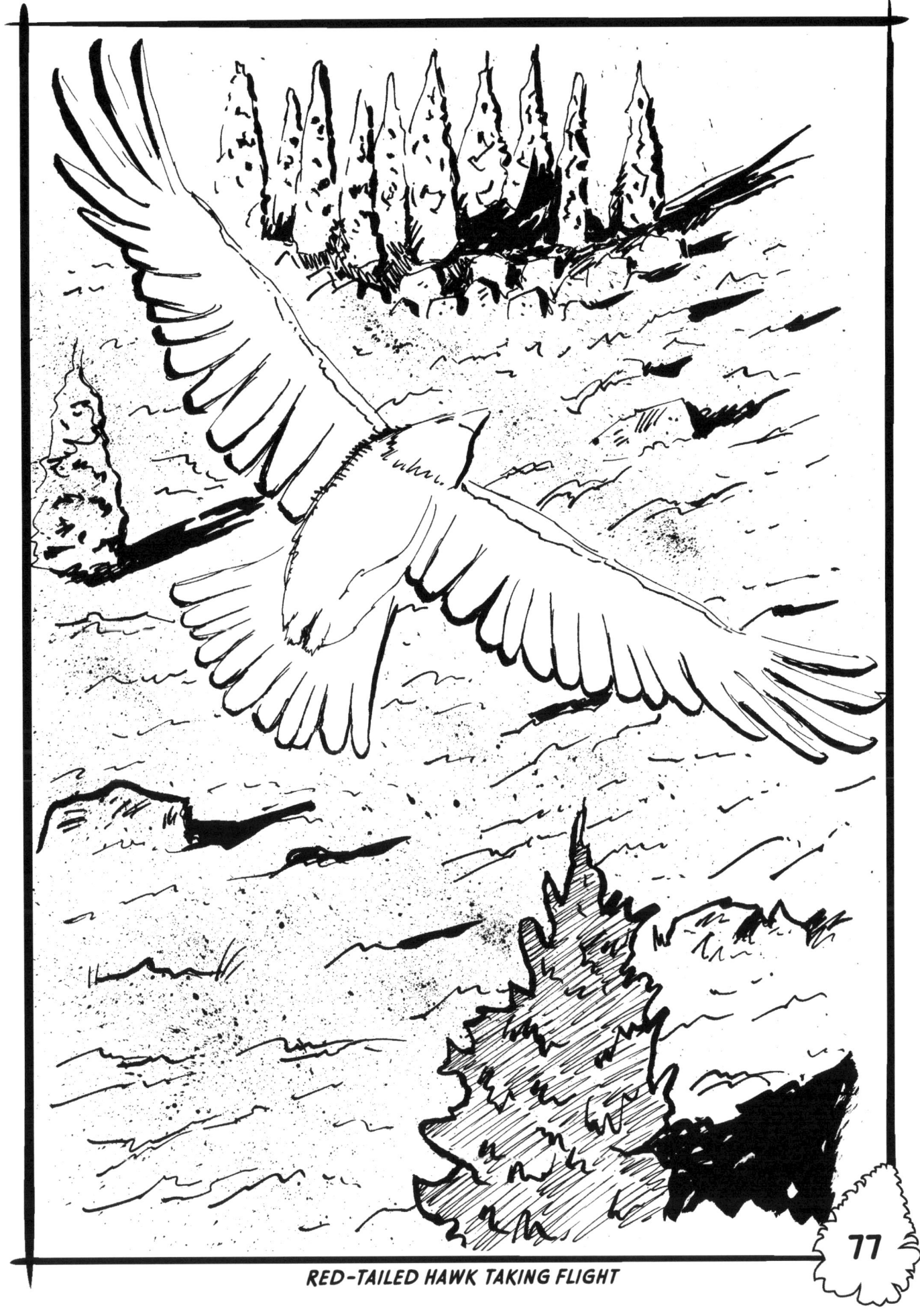

RED-TAILED HAWK TAKING FLIGHT

77

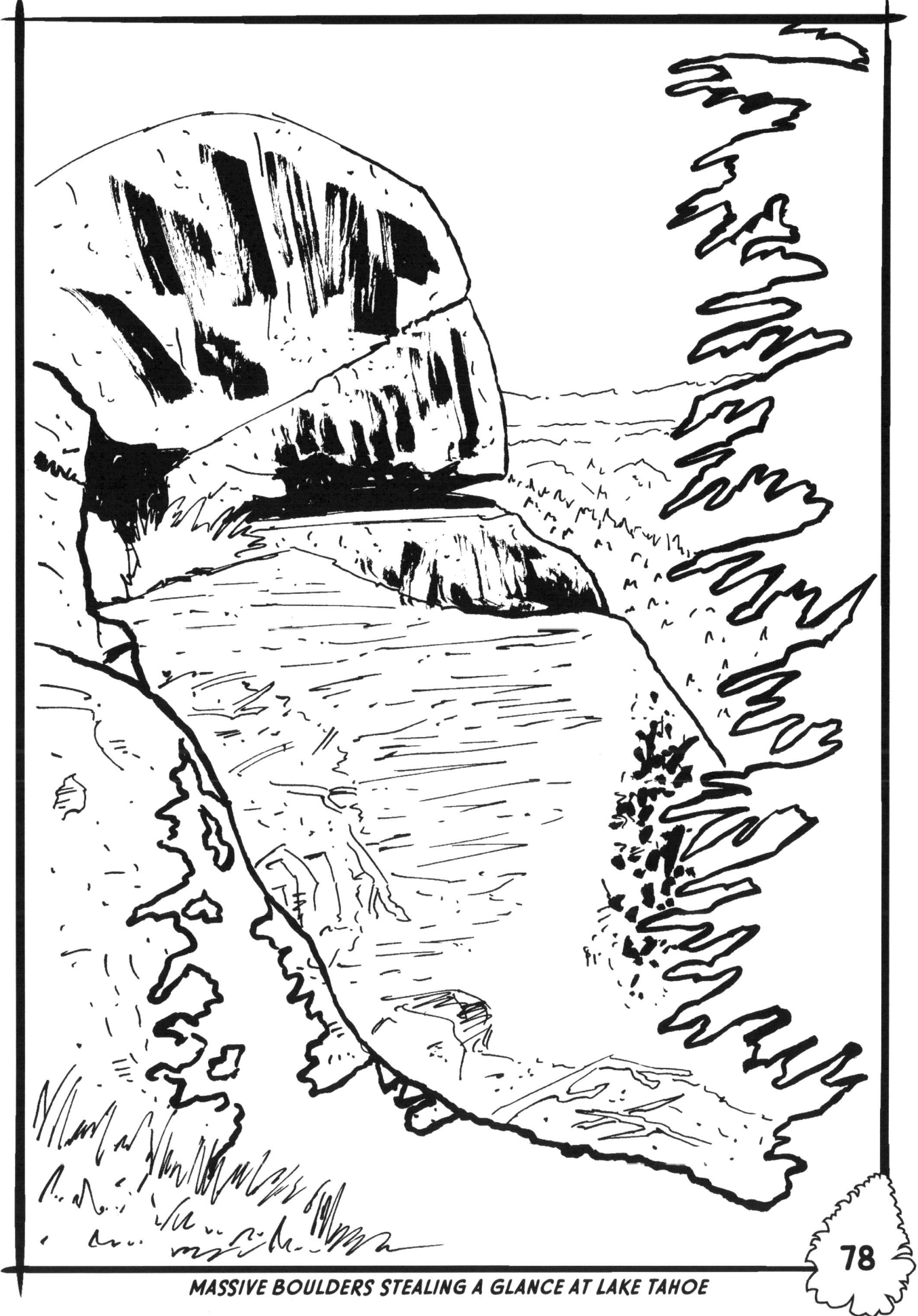

MASSIVE BOULDERS STEALING A GLANCE AT LAKE TAHOE

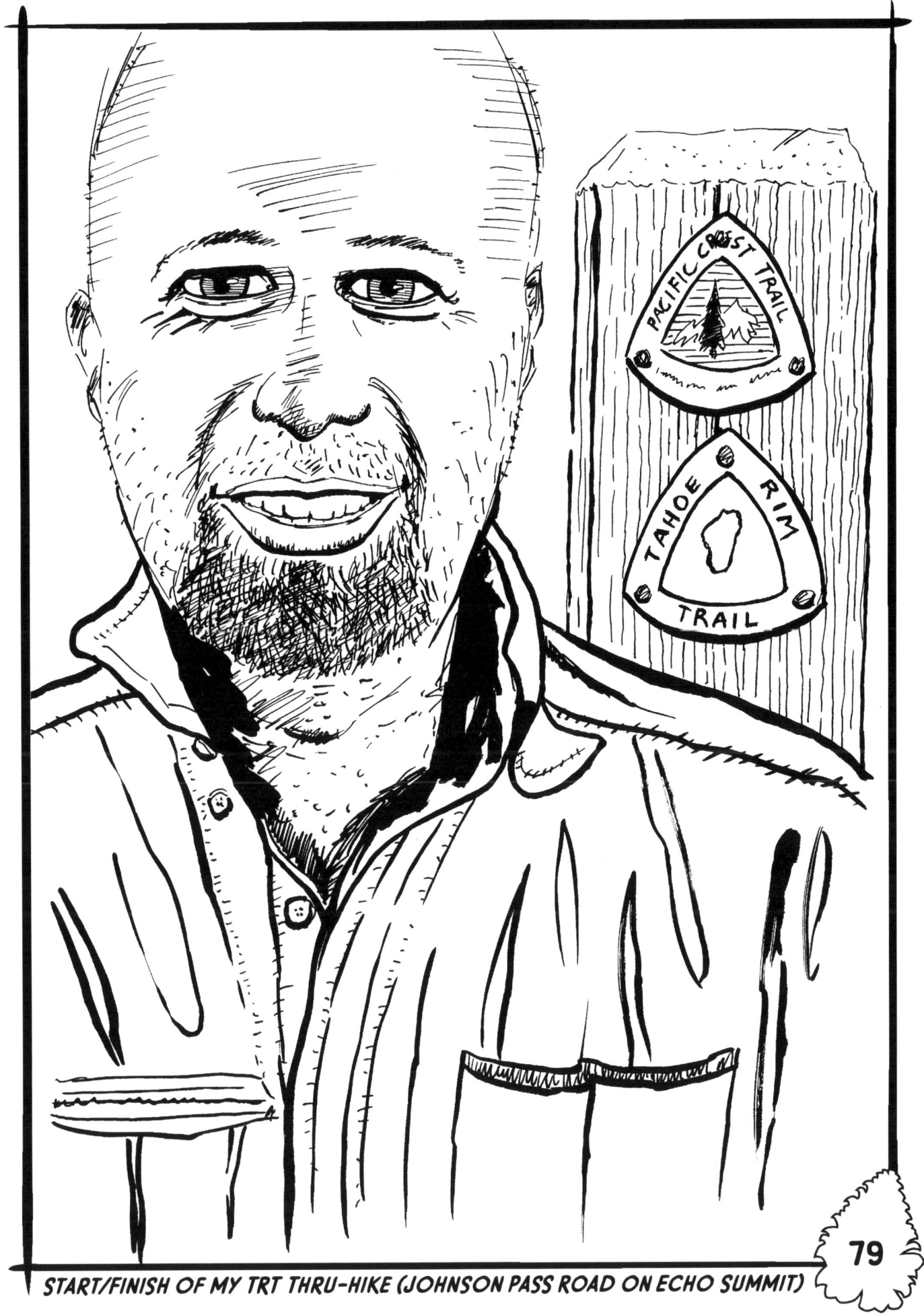

START/FINISH OF MY TRT THRU-HIKE (JOHNSON PASS ROAD ON ECHO SUMMIT)

Made in the USA
San Bernardino, CA
04 November 2016